Week-By-Week Coaching™ Presents….

MW01256944

WEEK-BY-WEEK GUIDE TO

COACHING

U-11 SOCCER VOL. 2 (Fall)

A VERY DETAILED PLAN FOR A FUN *AND* COMPETITIVE SEASON

SCOTT WHEELER

This book is dedicated to my awesome wife, Birgit, who has lovingly given me up for extended periods of time to coach and write. It is also dedicated to our daughter Ashley who has supported this effort in so many ways.

Contents

Introduction

About this Teaching Plan

First things first, because I respect your time. Is this plan for you? Given that the skill level of individuals and teams can vary so widely, this is my assessment of how useful this content might be for you. Though geared toward competitive soccer, I believe this teaching plan is wonderfully suited for any recreational team for the age-level indicated. I believe it would work well for any club team that plays in lower to mid-level divisions of their competitive leagues. If you are coaching a top-level team, you might find a few good training nuggets inside, but much of the content herein will likely be remedial for your players.

This teaching plan is different in many ways. Perhaps the most important difference is its respectful deviation from conventional guidelines regarding how to structure training sessions. While current convention calls for more 'free play', this plan leans in the opposite direction to deliver more structured teaching of skills. My early consumption of literature related to best-practices in coaching led me to the reinforcing belief of legendary UCLA basketball coach John Wooden. In his book Wooden on Leadership, Coach Wooden states, *"The primary reason I stopped using full-court scrimmages regularly once our season began was that I viewed them as an inefficient format for good teaching. Why? They wasted time. While players ran from one end of the court to the other, time was being squandered."* (Wooden and Jamison, 2005). The well-intended push for more free-play, at the expense of structured learning, has been to 'increase the joy' for the game. I believe that structured learning and joy for the game are not mutually exclusive and that many precious minutes are currently being lost to aimlessness. If you are up for a teaching plan that breaks with conventional wisdom and follows the principles of the most successful basketball coach in history, please continue reading.

Another significant difference is the level of focus and granularity that this teaching plan offers. When I first started coaching, I reached out to a couple of experienced coaches in my community for guidance. What I received back was surprising. Neither had any documented plans to speak of (or anything they were willing to share) and the response was not much better than, *"I do a little of this and a little of that."* This plan represents the antithesis of that response. This plan doesn't leave you hanging and instructs exactly what to teach during every minute of two 1-1/2 hr. practices per week for 9 ½ weeks. This doesn't mean that you have to teach this schedule, but it's a very pragmatic framework for you to adapt as you see fit. This is the plan that I wish I had on Day 1.

A philosophical difference you might find between this teaching plan and other references in the market, is its focus on training aggressiveness. If you are uncomfortable with the word 'aggressive', just substitute the word 'assertive.' Every coach loves to see the aggressive player show up on their team, but few seem comfortable teaching the behavior. After watching her first club team get pushed around on the field regularly, I resolved to personally help strengthen my own daughter's physical presence on the field. It worked. For the time that she was the same stature as recreational players I was coaching, I would offer the '$10 Shielding Challenge' at the beginning of the season. I would ask my team if anyone wanted to make $10 bucks by taking the ball from Ashley. With great excitement they all lined up, only to be thwarted by some of the best shielding technique that I have seen at the youth level. When asked if they would like to learn how to protect the ball like Ashley, they responded with equal excitement. Through this type of training, my assistant coaches (equally obsessed Dads) and I have produced spirited players that are able to protect the ball from competitors that are two heads taller.

One final way this book is different is the format in which it is presented. The physical format is larger and the font-size is larger for improved readability. This plan is NOT an exercise in fitting abbreviated content into the neat little boxes of a standardized 3-4 block one-page training plan. The format of this content is more free-flowing with a lot of diagrams and nuanced explanation of what you would expect to see in the process of teaching. For newer coaches trying to make sense of things, this nuance includes not just what to do, but also why it is being done and what type of fundamental behaviors are being trained.

About Me

I don't have the long pedigree that you might expect to find from someone publishing a book on youth soccer. Inspired by the reign of Pelé, I played soccer on my high school's first team back in 1978 and barely managed to 'Letter' as a senior. For the next 35 years I mostly enjoyed watching soccer. It wasn't until I watched our U-10 daughter's first competitive season unfold that I felt compelled to coach her in a different style of soccer. So, we took a step back from club and I volunteered to coach recreationally so that I could lead training and development. As a software developer by trade, I am obsessed with details and continuous improvement. As a Dad and coach, this is one of the most important (and satisfying) 'programs' that I have ever worked on.

Following our first awesome season, I went on to acquire my USSF 'E' License so that I could become a better coach. While this experience was valuable, and did help me develop better coaching technique, it wasn't fully what I was expecting. The course content was more about 'how' to train rather than 'what' to train... making the pursuit of a comprehensive training plan seem even more elusive.

At the time of this writing, our daughters have since moved on to play club ball in top divisions, but I have continued to coach recreationally because of the joy it brings me. In training my teams with the same zeal that I would commit to training my own daughter, I have had the satisfaction of watching many of my players eagerly graduate to more competitive environments.

About you

Perhaps you are a new coach or an unsuspecting parent that has been persuaded to coach your child's soccer team. If so, don't let your inexperience trick you into thinking that anyone with a day's more experience can do a better job. While it always helps to have some experience, you don't need to have star dribbling skills or be master tactician at the youth level to deliver an awesome experience to your team. A little bit of gray hair and a lot of enthusiasm will take you further than you imagine.

One truth that I have discovered, in both Select and Recreational soccer environments, is that no one is more vested in the success of their child than the parent coach. The first ingredient (and secret weapon) in achieving this success is being organized and having a good plan, be it this plan or a different one that you judge to be more appropriate for your team. Be careful to not underestimate the time that you will commit to preparation. If you do any instructional job correctly, it's easy to spend 3 or more hours preparing for every hour of new material being presented (Dashwood, 2012). Having a good plan frees you at the onset of the season to focus entirely on delivery.

Enthusiasm-in-delivery is the second ingredient that you bring to a successful season. Be vocal, enthusiastic, and demanding in teaching your team and they will reflect your energy. To quote Coach Wooden again, *"As a leader, you must be filled with energy and eagerness, joy and love for what you do. If you lack enthusiasm for your job, you cannot perform to the best of your ability. Success is unattainable without Enthusiasm."* (Wooden and Jamison, 2005).

Recommendations

If you are still reading, here are some recommendations for getting the most from this teaching plan if you decide to use it:

If possible, read it from cover-to-cover well before your season starts. Doing this gives you the full context of what is being taught in the beginning of the season and how it relates to skill progression by the end of the season. Digesting this material before you start will also trigger many mental notes related to equipment needs, support, and adaptations you might want to make.

Realistically, adhering to the minute-by-minute schedule indicated for each practice will be challenging, even for experienced coaches. Do your best to stay on track, but remain flexible. If your team is 'digging' a particular drill and you see that they are getting a lot of value from it, consider skipping something later in the schedule and maybe coming back to it. Just make sure that what you skip doesn't represent a significant dependency for skill progression (you only know this by reading ahead!).

If you are a recreational coach, I recommend picking the later time slot for practice. The reason for this is to remove any pressure to be off the field at a particular time to make room for another team. If you want to train for 1-1/2 hours (vs. standard 1 hr.) each practice, you can't do it if there is another team waiting to get on the field. Another benefit of the later time-slot is that it seems to remove pressure from parents to have their kids to practice on-time; this translates to better attendance and less hoop-jumping for you to make drills work. And perhaps the most important benefit of the later time-slot is to enjoy the glow-ball that brings a special element of fun to SSGs when the sun starts to set earlier in the Fall.

Ask for an even number of players on your roster, if possible. Assuming that most players will show up for most practices, there will be many partner-based exercises where you (or Asst. Coach) will need to pair with the odd player. This basically eliminates one coach from walking the drill and offering positive corrections to players. Corrections are an important part of improvement; if players don't receive feedback and correction, it's more difficult for them to improve. Anytime you eliminate 50% of these corrections, all players suffer. I consider a roster of 12 to be ideal for 9v9 play. 13 players will make things more difficult. 14 players is too many, but still better than 13.

If you are a recreational coach, and can only train one hour for each practice, consider carving out an appropriate ½ hour from each practice and offering an optional 1-hour practice on the weekend. This isn't ideal, but I have done this with younger groups and it has been very well received. If you do this, save the more tactical work and SSGs for regular practice and the foot skills and agility work for the optional practice.

Good luck with your season and I would love to hear from you if you end up using this plan to teach your team the game of soccer. You can reach me at WeekByWeekCoaching@gmail.com

The 6 Commandments of Every Practice
(until I can think of 10)

Setup Early - Minutes matter! Get to practice early to get your field setup. You have to treat time with the proper respect that it deserves. Master of time-management and former UCLA Coach John Wooden states about the use of time, *"As a leader, it is important to acknowledge that you and your rivals are essentially the same in this regard. Therefore, the contest comes down to who uses their allotted time to best advantage---who has the fewest missteps when it comes to building productivity into each moment of time."* (Wooden and Jamison, 2005).

Don't underestimate the number of extra touches and cycles in a drill that can be accomplished by better utilizing the minutes that tend to slip away. The single biggest thing you can do to respect time is to be prepared. This means having a plan, making sure that your assistant coach knows your plan ahead of time, being 30 minutes early, and making sure the field is laid out as completely/efficiently as possible so you are not measuring space and dropping cones throughout practice.

Practice with properly inflated balls – It's not enough to say, *"Bring a properly inflated ball"*, when instructing parents on how to prepare their child for practice. Most parents haven't a clue what 'properly inflated' means and most don't have ball pumps to correct the deficiency if they did. Practicing with a properly inflated ball is a necessity for training good 'first touch' and is often neglected in both Club and Recreational environments. As coach, you can bring your own ball pump to practice, but you can't afford the time for 12 players to sequentially drive 9 Lbs. of air into their #4 ball; you will never get started if you do. This is a requirement that should happen 'off-line' so that it doesn't impact the precious minutes you have for practice.

I recommend getting yourself an Under Armour Dual Action Ball Pump (plus a few extra needles) and recommending to your players' parents that they get one too. Encourage them to bring their pump to practice (labeled with their name) so they can share with teammates. You can find these on Amazon for about $20 and it's the best pump for the money that I have found.

Instruct your players to inflate their ball to **9 Lbs. of pressure** *BEFORE* they come to practice. Most kids this age find the whole operation of using the pump to be 'cool' and enjoy the responsibility. Your players are already going to show up with balls of different design, weights, texture, and quality, so remove the biggest issue of inflation as a variable so the ball-touch they develop is as consistent as possible.

Offer Rewards – Don't neglect the power of motivation. Have some type of reward that you can offer for the winners of the different little competitions you will have throughout your practices. In reality, everyone will get a reward, but the winners will get to choose first from what is available. I maintain what I call the 'candy stash' for this purpose. It's basically a thermal lunch box with lots of different options for your players to choose from. Just a quick survey from your players will let you know what types of treats they like. I even throw in a couple really high-end chocolate truffles to raise the stakes. Be sure to poll your parents at the beginning of the season to determine if you have any players with nut allergies; this will change the composition of your 'candy stash'.

Given that this plan targets the Fall season and temperatures of our first practices can easily hit 90 degrees-F, I have been known to bring individually packed slices of iced-down watermelon. If you want to see just how much energy your team has remaining after practice, tell them the largest pieces are on top and available for those that can get to them first! This means you need to be strategically positioned about 1/8 mile from wherever the cooler is.

Utilize Multiple Stations –   One of the single most important things you can do to prevent your training from devolving into unproductive chatter and inattention, is to minimize the amount of time that each player waits for time on the ball. This means setting up as many stations for the drills/exercises that you can so that wait-time is minimized. If you have to, engage a parent as needed to help maintain focus. With every team that I have coached, I have found at least one parent that was excited about being able help their child's team in this manner. While this only needs to be a behavior management role, you will be surprised at how quickly parents will become productive in mimicking the corrections that you give during drills.

Bring the Pressure - Let's face it, we all perform a little better under pressure. Whether it is running late through the airport like O.J. (reference for old farts) or scrambling to submit coursework before the midnight hour, pressure moves us to action. Soccer is no different. A common refrain in the competitive soccer community is to "Practice like you play." If you want your players to do this, you can't just tell them, you've got to design it into the very fabric of all your practices.   There is a time to bring pressure and there is a time for no pressure. While players are learning new skills, they should experience very little pressure. As they build some mastery, start to layer-in passive pressure. When they have a good grasp of what is being taught, add full pressure that would be characteristic of a real match.

Bring the Fun/Creativity – Periodically, try to participate in drills and exercises where it makes sense.   Your players are going love your involvement and you will have a blast. Participating in the occasional small-sided game (SSG) also allows you and your assistant coach to showcase the communications skills that you want them to learn. Years ago, I read a self-help book by David J. Schwartz entitled, The Magic of Thinking Big. One of his principles to live by that has stuck with me over time is, *"In everything you do, liven it up!"* (Schwartz, 2012).   With this in mind, don't be afraid to try new things and add your own twist to training to make it more interesting. Don't be afraid to lose your adult stuffiness and let the child inside 'come out to play.'

Practice 1-1 - Email and Pre-Work:

Hey Parents,

It's already time for us to start working together to maximize the benefits of our training. One important area of focus this season will be that of communication. Here is an Internet search reference to a short video by popular online trainer, Dylan Tooby of Progressive Soccer Training™, that explains just how important it is to communicate on the field:

YOUTUBE SOCCER SKILLS – HOW TO COMMUNICATE IN SOCCER – SOCCER TIPS (Tooby, 2015)

If you could please find this video and have your daughters watch this before practice tomorrow, it would be most appreciated!

Don't forget water! *It is going to be hot tomorrow and we will take plenty of breaks to stay hydrated. I recommend getting a 64 oz. (1/2 gal) well-insulated (Under Armour™) thermos versus the smaller uninsulated 25-32 oz. bottles that I have seen run dry on hot days. 64 oz. may seem like a lot, but you want to err on the safe side with water left over after practice and games. My personal mantra to my own daughters has always been, "It's better to have it and not need it, than to need it and not have it."*

Also, Assistant Coach [Name] and I have fun (yet value-added) activities before practices and your daughter won't want to miss them. We generally get to practice about 30 minutes early, so feel free to drop the girls early as we appreciate the extra time with them.

Thanks so much! If you ever have any questions, please feel free to reach out with a text or a call...I am quite accessible.

Thanks,
Coach Scott

Practice 1-1: Foot skills, off-ball support (4v0 Rondo), moving the ball quickly, and build-out Part-1

Welcome your players as they arrive to practice. In the age of COVID-19, you might risk a fist-bump (vs. hand-shake) or elbow-touch with players and their parents.

Introduce yourself to your players. Include in your message that you want to see them being bold on the field, taking chances, and being unafraid to make mistakes using the skills they will learn this season. Impress upon them that one of the new skills you will be working on is that of communication. Successful teams tend to be very vocal on the pitch. Players on successful teams are always communicating with each other verbally and non-verbally. Being a good communicator is NOT being bossy; it's being helpful to your teammates. Whether it's helping a teammate stay on-sides, reminding her to keep feet on the ground during a throw-in, marking an open opponent, or simply calling for the ball, good communication helps everyone get better and helps the team be more successful.

Ask by a show of hands how many watched the online video that was referenced in the 'pre-work' email? This will give you an idea of how committed the parents of your players are. If you get a show of just a few hands, and are doing a parent meeting after practice, bring this to their attention. Explain that you will be sending out important training and motivational materials throughout the season and that their support is important to their child's success.

Ask your players to raise their hand if they remember two points from the video and ask them to explain:

1) **Keep it positive** – Communication doesn't always have to be corrective in nature. For instance, if a teammate performs some skill well, complement her openly so that everyone can hear. Don't say things like, *"Don't be a ball hog!"*, but rather *"Let's work together to keep the ball. I'm here to support you when you run into pressure."*

and

2) **Be Specific** – Be specific in your communication to teammates. Rather than just yelling "Pass" or *"Mark"*, Let your teammate on the ball know that you are behind her for support. Or, point out an unmarked competitor for your teammate to cover.

Let them know that throughout the rest of the season you and your assistant coach will be challenging them to 'raise their voices' and be heard by their teammates.

Regarding weather, it can still be rather warm at the beginning of the Fall season. As a treat and motivator, I will often cut up and ice-down some watermelon for after practice. If you choose to do this to, you can raise the performance stakes by telling them, *"One way you can be first to get watermelon is to let me hear you communicate with your teammates. We will pick the two top communicators to be first in line after practice, and believe me, there are some pieces that are bigger than others. You don't have to be the biggest and fastest to be picked…just smart and vocal. Everyone else will have to run a lap at the end of practice."* Just listen to the communication that ensues!

(10 Minutes) Concentration – Start with a little bit of fun as the first warm-up. This game is played similar to the traditional card game 'Concentration', where players must remember the location of two-of-a-kind. This is a fun game that conditions players physically and they don't even realize it. This game requires large format cones to completely hide several different colors of matching pinnies.

So that nobody knows where the pinnies are, make sure you get to practice early to layout the game. Spread the cones out randomly with some far enough away to really make your players run. Set two cone-gates outside of the field-of-play for the two teams to queue behind and players to wait their turn. Between the starting cone-gates and the field, plant a 'coaching stick' in the ground for each player to jockey around (360 degrees) before they can go search for the pinnies. This adds an element of agility to the game and improves the warm-up.

Rules:

1. Leave your first cone turned over while you look for your second pinnie.
2. If the second pinnie is the same color, collect both pinnies and replace the cones.
3. Only one person from each team searching at a time. Next person can search as soon as teammate returns.
4. Be sure to turn the cones back over after each turn!

The winning team is the first to collect 3 matching sets of pinnies. Make the losing team do 10 push-ups.

(15 Minutes) Foot Skills - Setup a General Foot Skills Practice Area according to Figure 1-1. Have players align themselves between a set of cones to do their work.

(3 Minutes) Tick-tocks - Standard Tick-tocks (a.k.a. 'foundations'). Start with tick-tocks in-place. Focus on keeping knees bent. Progress to Tick-Tocks with 90-degree rotations. Make sure to turn in both directions. Graduate to tick-tocks moving forward. Have players start to split their attention between you and the ball to start training them to get their head up. Players that never learn to get their head up while dribbling will lose the ball to defenders that they never see coming. Randomly ask the players how many fingers you are holding up while they are moving the ball.

(5 Minutes) Outside/Outside/Inside Cut - This instruction begins to train one of the most effective, yet undertrained fakes in the game of soccer (my opinion) ... the change-of-direction cut back across the body. When executed properly, it leaves defenders moving in the opposite direction and can buy enough time to continue the dribble, pass to a teammate, or even get a shot off.

Start with the ball just slightly ahead and to the left of the left foot. Take two small touches on the ball with the outside of the left foot (shuffling sideways to adjust) then stretch the left foot all the way across the top of the ball and cut it back across the body.

Stretching the leg/foot across the top of the ball is the key to this move. Many players learning this skill will move their whole body to the opposite side of the ball and simply 'pass' it back to the opposite side with the inside of the foot. This is incorrect and it won't fake any defender. Make sure they are on the opposite side of the ball and reach over the top with their chopping foot to get the abrupt change of direction that fools defenders. They should use enough force to chop all the way across the body but not so hard that they lose control of the ball.

Do this side-to-side for the duration of this skill, making rounds to give positive reinforcement and corrections as needed.

(4 Minutes) Flamingos - When a comfortable level of mastery is attained, this skill can be used in turning the ball around a defender. This can occur when the ball handler is shielding (protecting) the ball and the defender overcommits across the body in her efforts to gain possession. Highly skilled ball handlers will actually 'bait' the defender across the body and take the ball behind their back in the opposite direction with this technique.

This skill is a basically a continuous pull-back around the standing leg. Ensure that ball is about a foot or so away from the body as it is being pulled around the standing leg.

To get your point across, do a short demonstration of why/how the 'Flamingo' will be used:

From a shielding position, with the ball behind and attacker in front, demonstrate how we want to keep/control the ball as far away from the attacker as possible. When the attacker tries to come around the front of our body, use the sole of your foot to pull it around your back to safety.

Coaching Points:

- Some players will try to pull the ball too tightly around the standing leg. Make sure there is adequate space to protect the ball from being poked away by the defender.
- Be sure to practice getting the forearm up and out to keep a defender at-bay.
- Watch for players trying to rotate the ball toward the front of their body (yes, it happens). You want to have them pull the ball around the back of their body as this supports more natural movement.
- Finally, ensure that the players are 'sole rolling' the ball from heel-to-toe and not side-to-side through the middle of their foot; this offers little contact and control of the ball. If you have to, physically reach down and turn their foot in the right direction so that it contacts the ball moves in the correct direction if necessary

(3 Minutes) Straight Dribble w/ Drag-Back Turn – Dribble side-to-side between cones. Focus on little touches using the laces or the 'pinky toe.' Practice first with the left foot only and then with the right foot only. Then practice touches with alternating feet with every step. Use a pull-back turn to change directions when you get to each side. This turn is also known as a 'drag back' turn.

There are some details to executing the pullback turn that are important. The turn should be executed with the same foot that that is being used to dribble and the body should turn so that it always faces the ball (i.e., pull-back with the left foot, turn to the left. Pull-back with the right foot, turn to the right). You will see some newer players actually turn in the wrong direction after they pull the ball back. This is wrong and needs to be corrected immediately. Upon turning, contact/control the ball with the outside of the foot **BEFORE** the foot hits the ground. Push the ball into space and continue in a fluid motion.

Internet Search Terms/Phrase for Skill Videos: SOCCER DRAG PULL BACK TURN VIDEO

General Foot Skills Practice Area

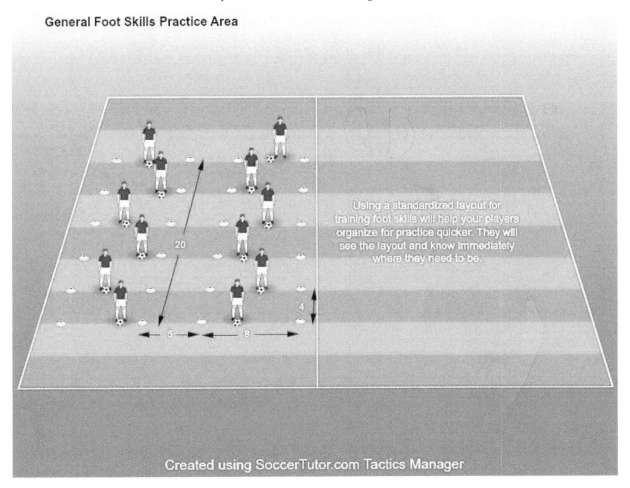

Using a standardized layout for training foot skills will help your players organize for practice quicker. They will see the layout and know immediately where they need to be.

Created using SoccerTutor.com Tactics Manager

Figure 1-1

(15) 4v0 Rondo – This drill trains the critical mindset of movement to support the player with the ball after making a pass. One of the most performance-limiting behaviors on the field is when a player takes herself out of the game thinking that her job is finished after she passes to a teammate. Rather than engage in a bursting sprint to support the receiver, she will downshift into 1ˢᵗ gear as if her leg of a baton-relay is finished. The exact opposite behavior is required for possession-based soccer. Get your players into the mindset of 'pass and move.'

So important is this mindset that best-selling author Dan Blank presents it as concept #8 of 53 in his first book Soccer IQ. Sometimes common-sense needs to be pointed out to us, and this is what Blank has done with what he has coined as 'The Three-Step Rule.' When a player passes the ball to a teammate, the natural tendency is for the nearest defender to pressure the receiver via the path of the pass, thereby cutting off the passer. This is why Blank states that the passer *"...must immediately transition from being a passer to being a passing option."* (Blank, 2012). His (commonsense) argument is that the passer needs to take at-least three steps to come 'out of the shadow' of the pressing defender to remain a passing option. 4v0 Rondo without pressure is the perfect structured tool for introducing this behavior.

Rondo 4v0

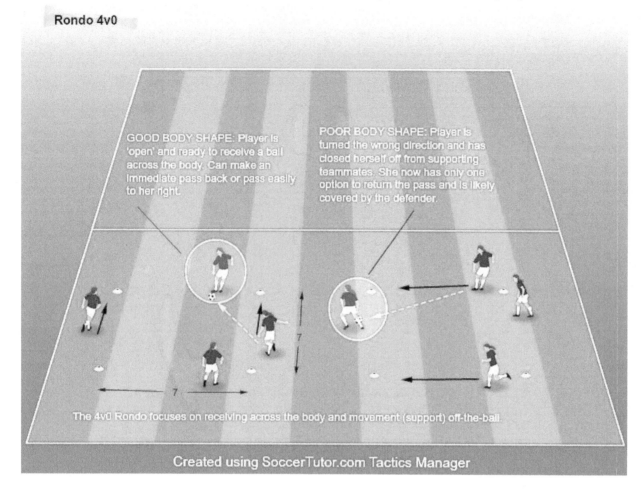

Figure 1-2

If you have been utilizing this training series, your players will have had a good introduction to basic Rondo (a.k.a. 'piggy in the middle') from the previous season. If you did not train 4v1 Rondo in the previous season, you can catch-up by researching this method using the Internet search terms below. Without the element of pressure, this drill takes a small step back to reinforce receiving with the proper foot, passing across the body, and supporting-player movement. Don't introduce any pressure by way of a middle defender at this point, but rather let the players start getting comfortable with the basic movement.

Lay out an appropriate number of stations for 4 players/each according to Figure 1-2. Keep in mind that an appropriate number of stations will also be dictated by the number of coaching resources you will have available to properly manage performance.

Do a demonstration with some of your better ball handlers to show how the movements are properly executed. Emphasize that, after making a pass, the supporting player needs to sprint toward the cone and have an open body shape that is ready to receive a pass back. 'Open' body shape means facing the inside of the square with the correct posture. During this drill, players may receive a pass back immediately and play can reverse direction. Allow less skilled players to take two touches when receiving, the first to control and the second to pass.

Run the drill for a few minutes and give as much praise and as many corrections as possible.

Adding an element of practicality: Stop the drill and do a small demonstration of why it is important to move all the way to the cone to support. Do this by positioning yourself as a defender inside the square and having an outside player make a pass to a teammate. Show how the defender will immediately close into the wake of the ball and eliminate a pass back if there is no movement.

Continue running the drill giving plenty of praise and corrections.

When your teams start to master the basic movement start slowly and steadily ratcheting-up the speed. Make it a game. See how many passes each Rondo can complete in a 60 second time period.

<u>Coaching Points:</u>

- Receive the ball across the body with the inside of the foot.
- Take two touches...the first to control and the second to pass.
- Move all the way to the corners to support.
- Players opposite each other should reflect a mirrored position with respect to support.

If you think this concept of ball-possession and support might be too complicated for this level of play, just check out this example of some U8s doing 4v0 posted by Vimeo user 'Madero.' Hopefully, this video will enjoy some longevity on the Internet as it shows what is possible at younger ages:

https://vimeo.com/116725396

Internet Search Terms/Phrase for Skill Videos: SOCCER 4v0 Rondo VIDEO

(25) Slalom Speed Dribbling - The team that moves the ball faster and plays with more energy has a big advantage over the team that doesn't. The sooner you can get your players conditioned to this mindset, the more success they will enjoy. This fun drill introduces the concept of taking bigger touches on the ball to maximize speed-of-play.

Equipment: You will need 12 (2 sets 6) coaching sticks, a stopwatch, 16 cones, and 12-14 pinnies of any color for the drill.

Layout the field as seen in Figure 1-3. Each station should be 3 slalom sticks in a row about 10 adult paces apart. Set cone gates another 10 paces from each end for the players to start and finish through. This gives you a solid 35-40 yards for them to drive the ball. This symmetry also allows them to dribble in the opposite direction. Setup four stations (if possible) adjacent to each other so the players can compete with each other on speed. These stations should be about 8-10 paces apart so the players are not dribbling on top of each other if their ball goes wide. The two inside stations should be lined up on the goal posts.

Slalom Speed Dribbling

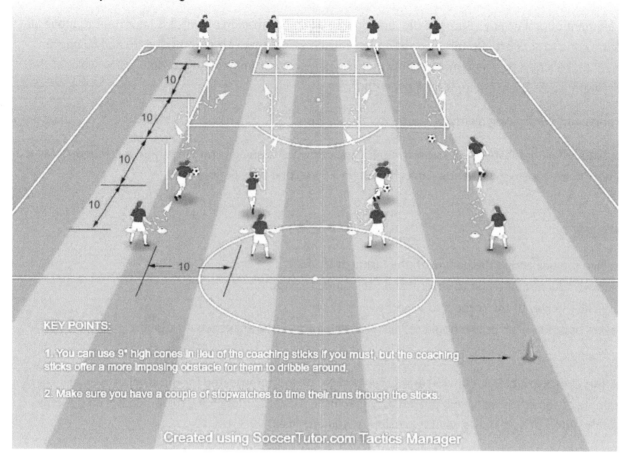

Figure 1-3

Begin with a simple demonstration of how you want them to dribble through the sticks. Don't worry about speed during the demonstration, but just show them starting, dribbling in and out of the sticks, and finishing through the gate at the other side.

Slalom Speed Dribbling with Pressure

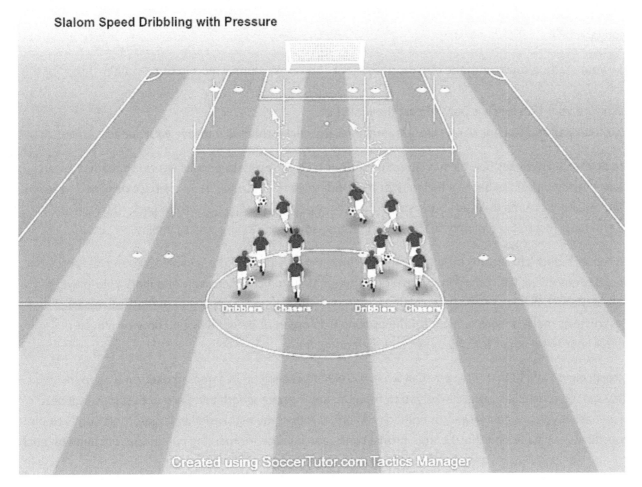

Figure 1-4

Send dribblers in individual waves; wait for each wave to finish before sending the next. Time each wave of dribblers through the sticks and see who can get the fastest time. Make a big deal out of the best time and challenge everyone to beat it. When all dribblers from one side have dribbled to the other, start the same process back in the opposite direction.

Give tips on how to get a faster time, like taking a big first touch past the first stick. Ask them, *"What do you think is the minimum number of touches to get the ball through?"* Ask them to try and take that minimum number of touches. Restart and see if you can get some better times and a new record.

Be sure to give them a water break in the middle of this drill as they are working very hard. During this water break, remove the outside stations so that only the ones in the middle remain.

After the break have the players that were on the outside stations line up next to the players on the inside stations without a ball as indicated in Figure 1-4. These players will become chasers. This adds an element of pressure to the exercise that motivates the dribblers to move faster. The chaser must follow the dribbler through the sticks and try to snatch the tail (pinnie) out of the dribbler's shorts. The chaser can begin after the dribbler clears the first stick. Have the chasers/dribblers switch roles after each pass through the sticks. Watch the times go down with the addition of the pressure!

Coaching points:

- Take your starting touch with the outside of the foot. This represents a more natural running form for the start.
- Make sure your first touch is big and past the first stick.
- Try to make all subsequent passes close-to and near the sticks; this will improve your speed.

(20) Intro to Stretch – There has been a movement underfoot by U.S. Soccer to encourage youth teams to start their attack by playing out of the back...a hallmark of the modern game. 'Stretch' is an exercise designed to teach players to immediately assume their attacking shape for the purpose of playing out-of-the-back. 'Stretch' is designed to train fast restarts and eliminate these competitive-advantage killing pauses in play.

Most youth soccer teams (club teams included) seem to 'hit the pause button' during goal kicks and Keeper distributions, thereby giving the competitor ample opportunity to organize defensively and mark your players. Upon collection of the ball by the Keeper, we want to train the whole team to engage in the fastest restart possible. Fast restarts make it more difficult for the opponent to organize defensively and provide a better opportunity for your team to get the ball out of their defending third.

If you are practicing on a field that is bigger than what you will be playing on in games, make sure you mark appropriately spaced touchlines. This allows you to train the appropriate length and pace of passes as will be required in games. If you are on a larger (or unmarked) field, layout some high visibility large-profile cones to mark the touchlines. I have found that 12 large profile cones are suitable for marking half of the touchline on each side.

Using Figure 1-5 (Stretch: Ideal Shape), lay out low-profile cones to mark the locations where each position should move-to in assuming the teams 'attacking shape.' Most importantly, ensure that the outside backs are positioned deep enough to draw the other teams' forward players into coverage. I encourage the outside backs to play even with the 6-yard line where the Keeper takes her goal kicks. Ideally, any passes intended for the LB & RB should not be directly to them, but rather slightly ahead of them (leading pass) to receive into space.

While this strategy recommends Outside Backs be deep and closer to the touchline, new rule changes (as of 6/19) allow teammates to be inside the penalty area. While getting wider provides greater advantage, you may need to take advantage of this rule if your Keeper has a weak kick.

Stretch: Ideal Shape

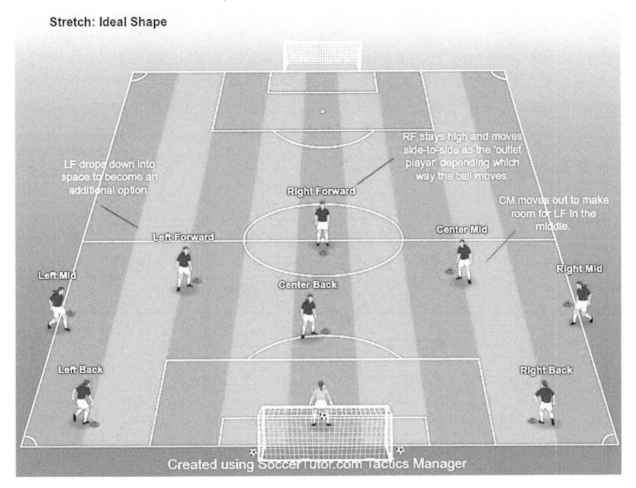

Figure 1-5

At the time the Keeper collects the ball (or it rolls past the end line), player positioning is typically condensed as indicated in Figure 1-6 (Out-of-Play); meaning that players are congested around the 18-yard box after an unsuccessful attack. The moment the Keeper collects the ball, everyone should be yelling, "*STRETCH!*". This is the trigger-word for the entire team to sprint to their pre-determined position in preparation for playing out-of-the-back. At this point, each player should be prepared to receive the ball on-the-run if they are fortunate enough to be unmarked. The faster the restart, the more likely it is that you escape your defensive half with little resistance. The first time your team does this in a game, you will notice a number of the other team's players actually walking with their backs to the ball...thinking that there will be the classic 'pause' associated with the goal kick.

Stretch: Out-of-Play

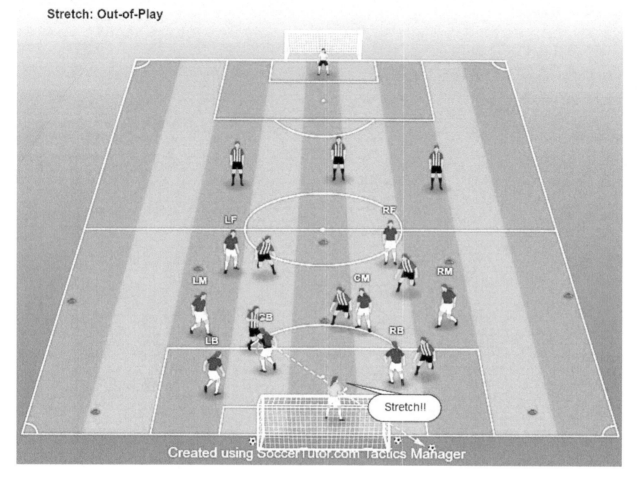

Figure 1-6

Make it a rule that, when playing a 3-3-2 formation, the Left Forward (LF) drops down as a 2nd layer receiving option and the Right Forward (RF) functions as the 'outlet' player staying high. The Center Mid (CM) shifts up and to the right of the RF. It is important that the RF not remain static and moves to the side of the field where the ball is expected to 'pop out' of the backfield. As seen in Figure 1-7 (Stretch: Organize Quickly), everyone should transition to an attacking shape to support the forward players.

Start with a couple of dry runs. Run the action multiple times with key players rotating in/out so that they can get some practice. This especially includes Goal Keepers as they are the initiators of the attack. Bring your players in tight to simulate consolidation, then yell "Stretch" to trigger the runs into attacking formation. Give the GK 3-5 seconds to find an open teammate and distribute the ball. Have them quickly roll the ball out to the L&R Backs and see how quickly they can get the ball to the outlet striker via the L&R Mids.

Stretch: Organize Quickly

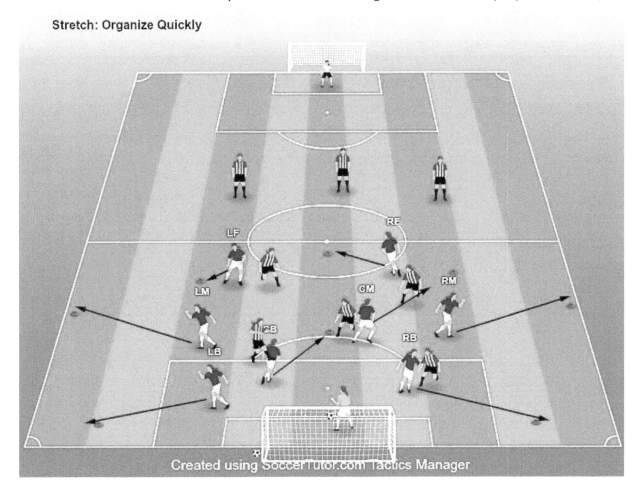

Figure 1-7

After your players are comfortable with the basic movements, introduce one or two defensive players in the consolidated starting position to add some pressure. Not too much pressure, but just enough to add a sense of urgency to the distribution. You will find that, initially, these one/two defenders are able disrupt play. With a little practice, your team will get better at getting the ball out.

IMPORTANT: Some might disagree with this strategy, but I recommend taking ALL goal kicks at the middle of the field at this level of play. See Figure 1-8 (Stretch: Catch Them Unprepared) for a few of distribution options that could present themselves. This positioning allows maximum spread of the field, thereby minimizing the coverage/marking by the opponent. If your Keeper moves the ball to a far corner of the box, everyone moves with her and individual competitors can then effectively mark more than one player. This also doubles the distance she has to pass to the other side of the field, if necessary. Taking kicks from the middle of the 6-yard box optimizes the length of any pass that the Goal Keeper takes.

Stretch: Catch Them Unprepared

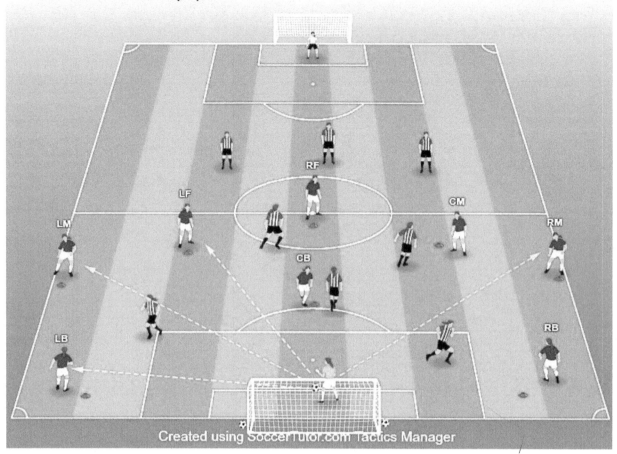

Figure 1-8

Prerequisites and practical considerations: This style of playing out-of-the-back is NOT going to work unless you have a Goal Keeper with a strong enough leg to get the ball out to the side with pace (speed). You need to quickly identify who this player (or players) will be and start training them immediately. If you have one player on your team with good hands and a strong kick, you are blessed. If you have two, that's about as common as unicorn. So, be ready to compromise a little as you train this strategy.

Coaching Points:

- Demand that your players hustle into position and not walk.
- Keep an open body shape for receiving.
- Ideally, 1st touch should be in the direction of the opponent's goal (Think leading-passes!).
- Never turn your back on the ball when you are moving into position. Keep an eye on your GK as you Quickly move into position so that you don't miss a pass. Look over your shoulder to keep an eye on the ball as it may be coming your way.
- Distribution should occur within 3-5 seconds of yelling *"Stretch!"*
- Be sure to incorporate the points in the Q&A (next section) email to parents.

Practice 1-2 - Email and Pre-Work:

Hi Parents,

Absolutely awesome first practice tonight! During the last part of the practice, we worked on a team tactic of 'spreading the field' and building out of the back as soon as the keeper collects the ball. After only 20 minutes of work, they looked amazing. When you see them play their first game of the season, you will hear them collectively yell 'Stretch!' and quickly sprint into an attacking formation. Get them to tell you about this tomorrow sometime.

Here are a couple of questions you can ask them:

Q: What does speed do to the competition?
A: It kills. It catches the competition unprepared.

Q: When you sprint into attacking formation, what should you also be doing?
A: Looking back for the ball...the keeper may be distributing to you.

Q: When the Keeper distributes the ball out to you, is it OK to pass backwards to your teammate?
A: Absolutely.

Q: If you are playing a defensive position, how many touches you should take on the ball?
A: Ideally, not more than two before you pass the ball forward to your teammate.

Next practice we will be working on some 'strength on the ball' exercises to raise each girls level of aggressiveness. Please have them watch the following short 4 minute video by Dylan Tooby on the importance of playing more aggressively:

https://www.youtube.com/watch?v=Sql9BdjHt6I

Internet Search Terms/Phrase for Skill Videos: Tooby How to be Aggressive in Soccer

Thanks, and as always, please reach out if you have any questions or concerns.

Coach Scott

Hi Everyone,

Just another quick note regarding practice outside of practice...

During the first 30 minutes of practice last night we worked on simple ball mastery exercises (a.k.a. foot skills) to improve your daughter's control of the ball in tight spaces. These were the names of the individual skills:

- *Tick-Tocks - simple side-to-side touches between the legs*
- *Tick-Tocks with 90-degree rotation - turn to the right or left after several side-to-side touches.*
- *Simple side-to-side movement - inside of right foot to move the ball to the left; Opposite in the right direction. keep body facing forward as if attacker on back.*
- *Cuts across the body - two touches with the outside of the foot followed by a cut across the body with the inside of the same foot.*
- *Tight dribbling - dribble with the instep with every step and pullback turn with the same foot.*
- *Flamingos - pull the ball around the standing leg using the sole of the foot. dribbling direction/rotation should be towards the back.*

Please encourage your daughters to work these skills at home during our non-training days as it will greatly improve their effectiveness on the field in the weeks to come.

Thanks,
Coach Scott

Practice 1-2: Foot skills, fake & finish, dribbling circuit, and strength on-the-ball

(-30) GK Catch and Bowling Distribution - As players show up to practice, play catch with those that are interested in playing GK. Show them how to properly distribute the ball in bowling-style fashion. Have them work on keeping their body relatively straight (perpendicular to the throwing direction) and control the ball by tucking it against their forearm. When they roll the ball out, it should be more of a fling across the ground unless the target player is close to them. The reason for this is to avoid, as much as possible, friction from the grass. As soon as the ball hits real grass, it starts losing energy as it travels. If you were on turf, it would matter less, but grass is a different animal...especially when the fields aren't cut as frequently as we would like them to be.

Have players not interested in GK simply pass with each other over longer distances to build their leg strength.

(-15) Chest Trap Practice/Competition – This receiving skill was introduced in the Spring. If you haven't trained this skill you can simply have players start long-passing with each other as they arrive to practice.

Split the players up into as many groups as you have coaches. They should form a queue, one behind the other. Using a two-handed underarm technique, the coaches will serve moderately arched balls to the player in the front of each queue. Practice at a distance of approximately 7 yards. Players move to the back of the queue after their turn receiving and passing the ball back to the coach. Give each player 3-4 turns. Coaches note who is executing the chest trap most effectively as there will be a competition between these players to determine who will compete in the 'Trap-Off' and be crowned champion.

When instructing the players to trap the ball, encourage them to control it as soon as it comes down so that no one else takes advantage of their brave and hard work. Do this no matter how far the ball might deflect in front of you by racing after it and passing back to the coach. If the ball drops in front of your feet from your chest, Congratulations! You have executed a perfect chest trap.

For the competition, start at a about 7 yards and increase the distance by two steps after each service. Coaches should be cheering on their competitor and encouraging her line-teammates to do the same. Be animated and pump-it-up! Yell things like, *"Go, [name]! Go [name]i! Team [name]!"* You will find that the players supporting will start cheering and some might even do a little dance! This builds camaraderie and ends up being quite a fun finish to some great training. Celebrate the champion mightily and with a round of applause.

It's all about motivation. Winner of chest-trap, pull-back, knock-out, and foot race get extra piece of watermelon.

(15) Foot Skills - Follow the diagram in Practice 1-1 for setting up the General Foot Skills Training Layout.

(2) Outside/Outside/Inside Cut - Reference basic from Practice 1-1. Continue practicing these basic movements that setup the inside chop move to beat a defender.

(2) Side-to-Side tight dribbling w/ Drag-Back Turn – Dribble between cones. Use left foot, then right foot, then both feet alternating. Make sure the ball stays close to the feet while dribbling. Players should be using the 'pinky

toe' area of the outside of the foot to move the ball. The touch should be more of a 'push' rather than a strike. The ball should remain only inches away from the foot in its movement.

(4) Shadow dribbling side-to-side while screening the ball - Have a player in the neighboring station leave her ball and take a position at the back of the player in front of her. The dribbler will simply move the ball side-to-side between cones (not moving forward) while screening the ball. Her body should be facing forward to effectively screen the ball while dribbling side-to-side. For now, use only the inside of the feet to dribble and change directions. The shadowing player should be studying and responding to the movement of the ball. The dribbler should be glancing over her shoulder to track the shadowing player.

(3) Flamingos - Reference basic drill from Practice 1-1.

(4) Pull-back competition – Map out some arbitrary distance or circuit and run a competition. Let's see who has been practicing. Offer some reward to the player that wins the competition. Emphasize that you don't have to be the biggest or toughest to win this competition; only the most skilled. You can pull-back any way you like, using one leg or both legs alternating.

(30) Inside Cut and Finish – This drill is designed to give your players an early opportunity to use an Inside Cut to beat a passive defender and take a shot on goal. Most club teams of this age will have some experience using the Inside Cut, but if you are coaching a recreational team, these first two practices could be their first exposure to the move. With this in mind, use the following progressions according to the skill-level of your players. This exercise should also give you an idea of which players might be well-suited to playing effectively in the forward positions.

Setup your practice field according to Figure 1-9 (Inside Cut and Finish Layout). To keep the diagram simple, only one side of the field is indicated with measurements. Make sure you setup a mirror-image of the layout on the opposite side so that players can train both feet.

The critical aspect of this drill is the realistic 90-degree close-down by the passive defender. The Inside Cut back across the body is most effective when attacker and defender are converging at an angle of 90-degrees (or less). The more acute the angle, the more difficult it is for the defender to adjust to the attacker's cut back across the body. While the defender is 'passive', this doesn't mean that they will be slow. Through the following progressions, this drill is ultimately intended to be executed at game-speed:

Inside Cut and Finish Layout

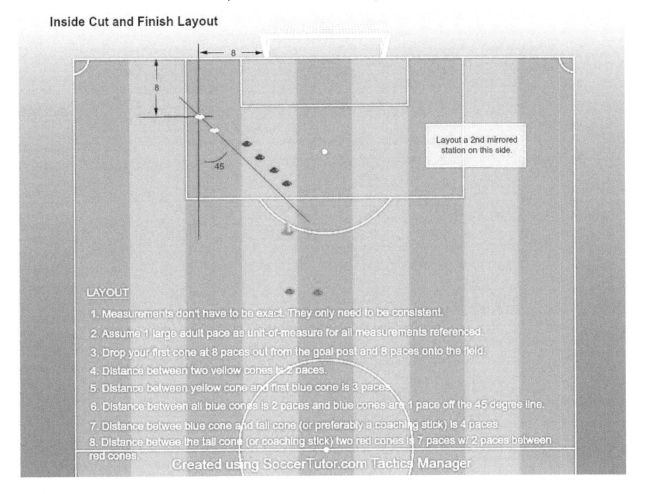

LAYOUT

1. Measurements don't have to be exact. They only need to be consistent.
2. Assume 1 large adult pace as unit-of-measure for all measurements referenced.
3. Drop your first cone at 8 paces out from the goal post and 8 paces onto the field.
4. Distance between two yellow cones is 2 paces.
5. Distance between yellow cone and first blue cone is 3 paces.
6. Distance between all blue cones is 2 paces and blue cones are 1 pace off the 45 degree line.
7. Distance betwee blue cone and tall cone (or preferably a coaching stick) is 4 paces.
8. Distance betwee the tall cone (or coaching stick) two red cones is 7 paces w/ 2 paces between red cones.

Created using SoccerTutor.com Tactics Manager

Layout a 2nd mirrored station on this side.

Figure 1.9

(5) Demonstration: Show your players what you want them to do. Start at the attacker's cone-gate at the top of the field. Dribble at a moderate pace past the coaching stick and change direction toward the yellow cone. You can simply drag the ball with the inside of the, or more experienced players can execute a Lunge Fake the first cone (or coaching stick). Once past the last blue cone, execute an Inside Cut across the body in the direction of the goal. Then, taking no more than one touch, take a shot on goal. If you can cut the ball back across the body with enough force, you can take the shot without the extra touch.

(5) Progression 1: Start with attackers only (no defenders). Have them dribble/execute at a moderate pace where they can control the ball. Split your players into two attacking queues and stagger their starts. Have them retrieve their ball after their shot and switch to the other line so that they can practice with the other foot. Rotate any players that want to play Goal Keeper so that they can get some practice fielding shots.

(5) Progression 2: Position 2-3 players at each post to serve as passive defenders. These defenders must keep a hand on the post until the attacker's body clears the coaching stick on her run. Keep the pace moderate at this point and instruct the defender that she should time her run in such a way that she reaches the yellow cone-gate at the same time the attacker clears the last blue cone. Players will now start to rotate clockwise through the two stations.

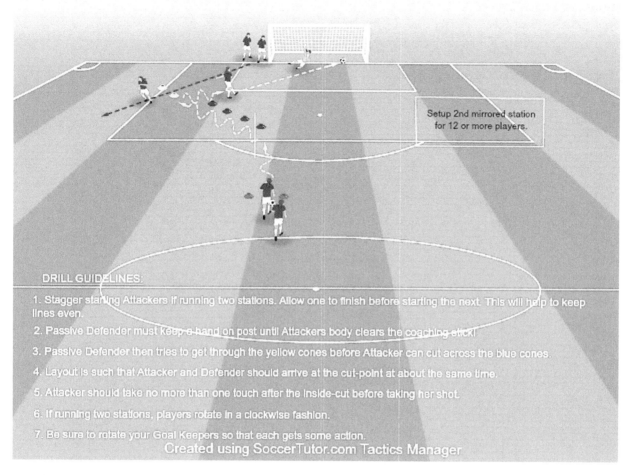

Setup 2nd mirrored station
for 12 or more players.

DRILL GUIDELINES:

1. Stagger starting Attackers if running two stations. Allow one to finish before starting the next. This will help to keep lines even.

2. Passive Defender must keep a hand on post until Attackers body clears the coaching stick!

3. Passive Defender then tries to get through the yellow cones before Attacker can cut across the blue cones.

4. Layout is such that Attacker and Defender should arrive at the cut-point at about the same time.

5. Attacker should take no more than one touch after the inside-cut before taking her shot.

6. If running two stations, players rotate in a clockwise fashion.

7. Be sure to rotate your Goal Keepers so that each gets some action.

Created using SoccerTutor.com Tactics Manager

Figure 1-10

(15) Progression 3: Time to step it up! Instruct the attacker and defender that it is now a race. The defender is now trying to clear the yellow cone-gate before the attacker can perform her Inside Cut. This final progression gives the attacker the realistic context of a defender closing, but allows her to practice the skill without interference.

Coaching points:

- Ideal cut will be forceful enough to move the ball across the body but not so hard that control is lost. This means not more than several feet past the body.
- Ensure that the attacking player is keeping the ball on the outside foot, away from the converging run of the defender...this sets her up for the chop back across the body.

(25) **Forward-Fake Dribbling Circuit** – A dribbling circuit presents a structured way for your players to develop ball control, rhythm, and a sense of timing in executing their fakes. What makes this a 'forward fake' circuit is the angle of take-away relative to the attacker. This training segment will be teaching the 'Lunge Fake', which has the dribbler taking the ball away in a forward direction and at an angle of approximately 45-degrees to the defender. This layout is designed for the type of move being trained...so it shouldn't be changed from what is specified. Specifically, don't make the mistake of laying out right angles (90-degrees) because it is easier.

Forward Fake Circuit

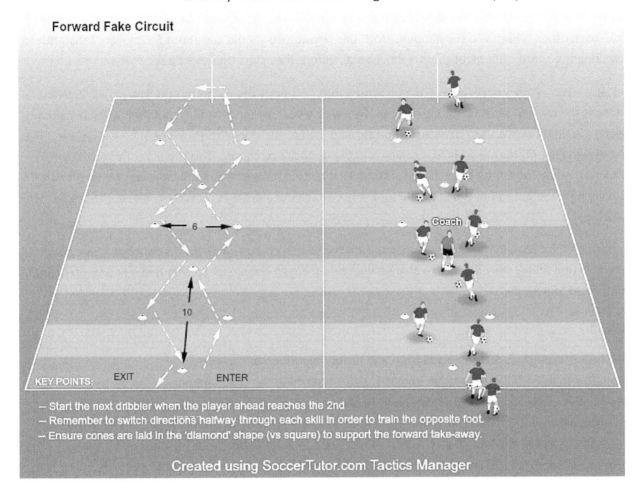

Figure 1-11

Using Figure 1-11, setup a 10-cone circuit where the distance between the four center cones is approximately 10 adult paces and each pair in-between is evenly spaced at 6 paces apart (3 paces off centerline). This will give the players sufficient room for 'tight' dribbling leading up to each fake. I recommend using high-visibility (yellow) and high-profile (tall) cones that represent a slightly more imposing obstacle to prompt the fakes. Players are more likely to execute fakes late if using the standard profile cones. Also, the end-cone doesn't support a 'forward fake', so you want your players to simply dribble around that cone to start their work on the way back. Consider posting a coaching stick on this cone to enforce cleaner turns.

(5) Demonstration - To acclimate them to movement through the circuit, have them all run with you through the circuit, calling out, *"Dribble, dribble, dribble, Fake!"* Tell them that they are to make their turn before getting to the cone, as each cone is a Defender looking to steal their ball.

Next, do a short demonstration through half of the circuit simply using the inside of the foot to change directions. When finished, have the players queue up at the end of the circuit. <u>If you have dribblers that you know are slower than the rest of the pack, make sure that they start at the end of the line. Otherwise, they will hold-up the group rather quickly.</u>

(10) Simple Change of Direction – (Remember to reverse direction after 5 min.) - Start sending them through the circuit to execute a simple change of direction with the inside of their foot. Start the next player when the player

in front of reaches the second cone; this should allow a reasonable amount of space between players so that they don't overrun each other...which will still happen. With this circuit, you should see about 5-6 players constantly in the queue waiting their turn. This gives them a short break before they start their next pass.

(10) Lunge Fakes – (Remember to reverse direction after 5 min.) - Quickly review/demo the Lunge fake with them. The Lunge fake is the most basic of fakes and most players with a year (or more) under their belt will have already been exposed to it. Start with a short demonstration through half of the circuit to show them how it is done. The key to effectively pulling-off the Lunge fake is selling it in the opposite direction. This is where the word 'Lunge' comes in...taking a really convincing lunge (step) in the fake direction before taking the ball away in the direction of the next cone with the outside of the opposite foot. I like to tell my players to, *"Lead her away, then make her pay."*

Send them through the circuit in the same manner as with the simple change of direction dribbling. Give equal amounts of correction and praise. Be sure to change direction through the circuit so that they get practice using their non-dominant foot.

Coaching points:

- Keep it slow enough to practice good form and proper execution at this point.
- Emphasize that the fake needs to be executed before reaching the cone and not on top of it.
- Position one of the coaches straddling the third cone as passive defender to give guidance, corrections, and encouragement. There is no substitute to having an actual body to dribble against. The coach can even feign following the fake to give the dribbler a feel for how the defender is supposed to move.
- More experienced players can use an advanced turn around the coaching stick if they desire.

(10) **Bulldozer** – This is another exercise designed to bring players (especially girls) 'out of their shell' and get them used to the physical contact common in the game of soccer. The coaches hold (American) football-style strike-pads and have players individually take turns driving them out of a small area. Players start with the shoulder, then push off (not shoving) to create separation, then shielding with the forearm, and finally driving the pad-holder out of a small area with their backs. Using a strike-pad as an intermediate object makes them more comfortable with being aggressive. You wouldn't be able to train this level of aggression without it. Most girls of this age have never done anything like this and you might just be surprised by their intensity.

If you don't have access to a commercially produced strike-pad as pictured, borrow a big seat cushion from your old couch.

Setup a small square with sides of about 3 paces according to Figure 1-16. Have one player just outside the square to start and the coach just on the other side of the line waiting to start.

Figure 1-12: Ready Position

Figure 1-13: Shoulders

Figure 1-14: Shielding

Figure 1-15: Back

On the command, "GO!", start with shoulders from a distance of approximately 1-2 feet so that we don't train a 'barge' per se. After a couple of seconds, give the command to, "PUSH OFF!". Be careful that the push-away doesn't resemble a shove as it will more likely result in a foul being raised. The goal is to make space in order to get the shielding forearm up and get side-on. Immediately after that, give the command to "SHIELD!" After a couple more seconds, give the final command of "BACK!" The player should then transition into low stance pushing backward with the back. At this point, and very importantly, the hands must be spread wide and wrapped around the defender (but not grabbing) to the degree possible to keep them from getting around to the (phantom) ball. To be clear, you are not using a ball with this drill. Make sure the players straighten their arms down and back and have them imagine that they are bars of steel. Tell them to clench their fists as this helps with strengthen their posture.

Bulldozer

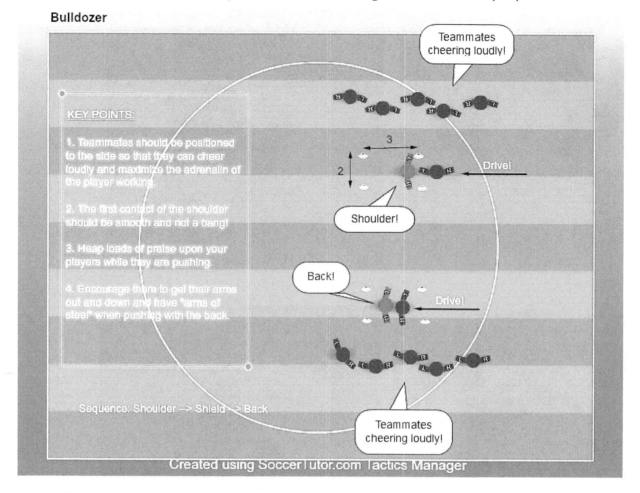

Figure 1-16

Instruct them to get loud as they push the pad as it gives them energy. Caution them that yelling, growling, and grunting (maybe), won't be tolerated in a game and are only for this training. Get them amped-up afterward by gathering them around and have everyone do their best 'Hulk' impressions, coaches included! This went over very well with my team and you should have seen the looks on the faces of other youth teams in the vicinity that were compelled to stop and watch what was happening.

Arrange the players in such a way that the ones not on the pad are facing their teammates on the side. For instance, if the player driving the pad has her left shoulder in the pad, make sure her teammates are on the side that she can see and hear maximum support. Small details like this are critical to maximizing assertiveness.

(10) Knock-Out - This is a simple game designed to promote strength-on-the-ball. Players will use the shielding ball-protection skills they have developed from the previous session (and season) to compete in the knock-out game. If you have players without experience in shielding, pull them along with an ever-so-brief demonstration and then get going.

You should already have a circle of 20-yards diameter setup and ready to go. See Figure 1-17 for the simple setup. If you have access to a full-sized field, and it is already lined, you can use the center circle for convenience.

Knockout

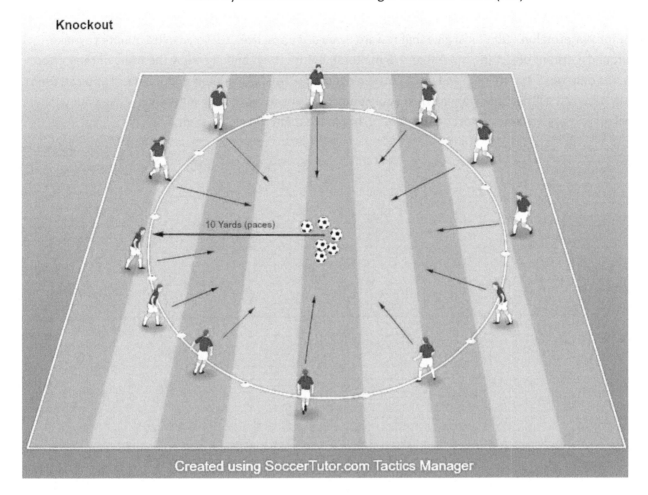

10 Yards (paces)

Created using SoccerTutor.com Tactics Manager

Figure 1-17

Place half as many balls as there are players in the middle of the circle. Position players evenly around the circle. On the whistle (or yell, *"GO!"*), the players race to take possession of a ball in the middle and retain possession using good shielding skills. If they don't immediately win a ball, they try to win a ball from a player in possession. This is a <u>shielding exercise,</u> do not allow them to dribble with the ball! If they dribble, or otherwise carry the ball out of the circle, they are disqualified from that round of competition and must give up their ball. Whistle stop after about 20 seconds. Vocally count-down the remaining 10 seconds to create a sense of urgency amongst those players without a ball. Those without a ball at the end of 20 seconds are out. Repeat the process until a winner emerges. Play as many rounds as time permits.

Stress to your players that shielding is not always pretty, but as long as it gets the job done, it doesn't matter what it looks like. Encourage the defenders to use shoulders and arms to move the attacker. Encourage the defenders to stab at the ball between the attacker's legs from behind if she stands square...anything goes! Just do everything you can to get the ball. The only other rule is that there can be only one defender per attacker. Too often there is one player with a ball smiling because no one is paying attention to her! Give the competition some stakes, tell them that the 3 finalists get an extra piece of watermelon (or whatever treat you are offering for the day) after practice.

Final Sprint for Watermelon - Don't just give that reward away after practice. Leave an extra minute to make them run around a distant object (no more than 1/8 mi. total) before they can fully enjoy the fruits of their efforts. Remember, it's only week 1 of training and most of them need work to improve their endurance. If you can train your team to have just a little more stamina than your competitor, it can make a big difference. Give your winners of individual drills/exercises a head start on the reward, but make them run all the same.

Practice 2-1 - Email and Pre-Work:

Hey Parents,

Another really good practice last evening. A few things we have been working on are:

1) Cutting the ball back across our body to beat a defender
2) Keeping the ball close to our feet when we dribble
3) Being strong on the ball (i.e., shielding and protecting the ball)

Here is a link to 9 minutes of inspirational video that shows Lionel Messi, arguably the greatest soccer player of all time, doing all three of these (and much more!). We can't be Messi, but if we emulate Messi just a little bit, we can greatly improve our game!

If you could set you daughter down to watch this video, and point out the skills they are learning at the times indicated, it would be most appreciated.

Watch for these skills at the following points in the video:

5 Examples Why You Shouldn't Make Messi Angry • Never Mess With Messi

https://www.youtube.com/watch?v=5bZQzPayuKU

1) @ 1:10 Messi cuts across the body and fakes his opponent to the ground.
2) @ 2:50 See how close he keeps the ball to his feet with fast/light touches
3) @ 4:00 Watch amazing strength on the ball as he battles multiple opponents for possession.

As a bonus, @ 5:23 there is great footage of an opponent effectively defending Messi (for a short time) with classic technique, which is:

1) Don't rush in... stay back a few feet.
2) Get 'side-on' so that you can better adjust to the movement of the attacker.
3) Wait for the attacker to make the first move...that's her job and not yours!

Thanks,
Coach Scott

Practice 2-1: Foot skills, up-back-through, tactical throw-in, and 4v4 SSG

If your field hasn't already been marked, make sure you lay out some large profile cones to indicate the touch lines (side lines). This lets players gauge where they should be relative to their playing positions. This is particularly important when you are teaching them to spread the field.

(-30) Dribble the Coaches – Setup two lines dribbling the coach, similar to the 'chop' session the previous week, but players will perform a simple lunge fake in this exercise. Lay your field out according to Figure 2-1. Coaches offer passive resistance to help build timing and do little more than follow the dribbler's feint opposite the take-away direction. Take-aways should be to the inside with an immediate shot on goal. The attacker then goes to the back of the opposite line to work the opposite foot. This is a good opportunity to start giving anyone that wants to play Goal Keeper a little bit of action. Have these players take turns in the Goal taking shots from the attackers. It is highly recommended that any player serving as Goal Keeper get a proper fitting pair of gloves to protect her hands. Make sure your Keepers are also getting some practice dribbling and taking shots. After a dribbling Keeper takes her shot, she assumes responsibility in the goal; The other Keeper then rotates out to dribble/shoot.

(-10) Practice throw-ins with a partner – Have players pair off with about 15-20 yards between themselves. Have them practice throw-ins and correct each other's technique where necessary. Try to pair players with somewhat equal throwing skills and have them stretch the distance between themselves. Walk around and ask them individually what good technique should look like and help them if they don't know.

(20) Foot Skills - Setup a General Foot Skills Practice Area according to Figure 1-1. Have players align themselves between a set of cones to do their work.

(3) Outside/Outside/Inside Cut - Reference basic drill from Practice 1-1.

(2) Tight Dribbling w/ Pull-back Turn - Reference basic drill from Practice 1-1.

(5) Side-to-Side Dribble w/ Shadow - Start by having players individually dribble side-to-side using the inside of their foot. Continue using the inside of the foot for now. Then have the players shadow their neighbor while they are dribbling. Make sure they are glancing over their shoulder to see where the defender is on their back while they dribble. Start using the language 'check your shoulder' to encourage this behavior.

(10) Step-Overs (In-Place) – Step Overs are one of the most useful moves in soccer to fake a defender and buy time on the ball. The introduction of the step-over is a prelude to other progressions that will improve effectiveness in changing directions (to avoid pressure) or turning the ball with an attacker on their back.

Dribble The Coaches

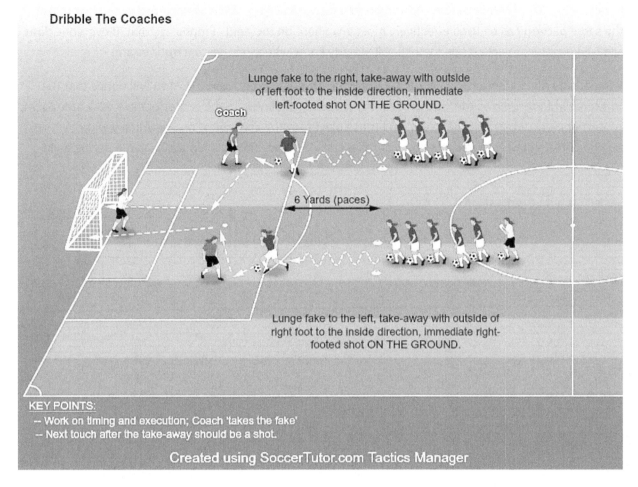

Lunge fake to the right, take-away with outside of left foot to the inside direction, immediate left-footed shot ON THE GROUND.

Coach

6 Yards (paces)

Lunge fake to the left, take-away with outside of right foot to the inside direction, immediate right-footed shot ON THE GROUND.

KEY POINTS:
-- Work on timing and execution; Coach 'takes the fake'
-- Next touch after the take-away should be a shot.

Created using SoccerTutor.com Tactics Manager

Figure 2-1

Start at the soccer ready position (knees bent, feet about shoulder width apart, and on the balls of the feet) and the ball centered and a few inches forward of the toes. Demonstrate the big sweep completely around the front of the ball from outside toward the inside. The sweeping foot should end-up all the way on the other side of the ball as well as being completely behind it. Body posture after a successful Step Over should only look like you have shifted left or right. So that your players sweep far enough around the front of the ball, tell them that the bottom of their cleats should brush the top of the grass.

Use the reference cited in the next parent email to study and deliver the Step-Over instruction, or, simply search using the following Internet search terms:

Internet Search Terms/Phrase for Skill Videos: SOCCER VIDEO HOW TO DO THE STEP OVER MOVE

Foreshadowing note: The introduction of the step-over is a prelude to other progressions that will allow players to be confident receiving the ball under pressure and turning with an attacker on their back.

FOOT SKILLS COMPETITION: If time permits, hold a quick step-over competition to determine the 1st person to get an extra piece of watermelon. See who can do the most *proper* step-overs in 30 seconds.

(25) Up-Back-Through - This drill represents a pattern of passing that is designed to support building out of the backfield this season (a lá 'Stretch!'). Start conditioning your players' minds to the tactic of passing the ball up, passing it back to support, and then sending it through to a forward player. While well-suited to building out-of-the-back, the same pattern can be used effectively most anywhere on the field. Emphasize that, if everyone does their job, and is in position, the player on the ball will already know where her passing options are.

Begin by laying out the field according to Figure 2-2 (Up-Back-Through: Progression 1). You will notice that the configuration somewhat resembles the 'Stretch!' configuration. The players in the center behave as Center Backs, those on the corners function as Outside Backs, and those players at the cone gates are essentially wide Midfielders. The pattern closely represents how your players will be positioned in an actual game during build-out.

Up-Back-Through: Progression 1

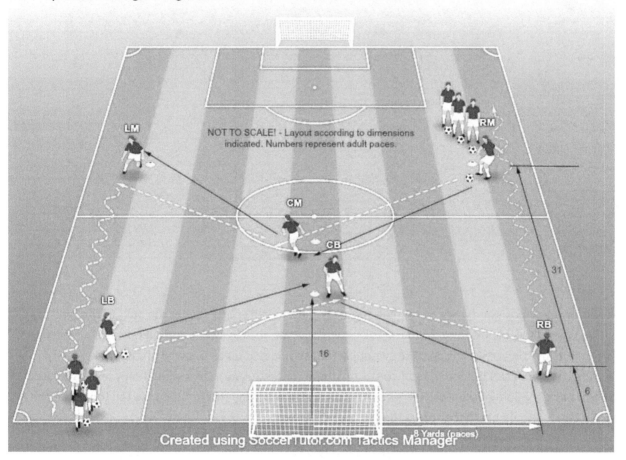

Figure 2-2

Run this drill in two progressions:

Progression 1 – This drill has two balls moving at the same time and starts in the counter-clockwise direction. In this progression, the players in the Right-Midfield and Left-Back positions start the sequence at the same time by making the pass '**UP**' indicated. The Center players receive those passes with one controlling touch and their next pass is '**BACK**' to the outside players. In similar fashion, the outside players take their first touch in the forward direction and dribble '**THROUGH**' to the to the opposite corner as fast as she can. This drill is all about taking big touches to move the ball quickly. During this dribble, players need to be using one foot, the one closest to the touch-line when they dribble. The purpose of using the foot closest to the touchline is to keep the ball as far away as possible from a Defender that may be pacing with them. They should also be using the outside of the foot to dribble. Before you switch to 'Progression 2' Make sure you switch directions so that they can get some practice dribbling at speed and passing with their opposite foot.

Players follow their passes to the next position in the sequence. The player in the front of the line may start the next passing sequence as soon as the outside players start their dribble in their direction. This keeps everything moving in a timely manner.

Time the dribble from the Left-Back and Right-Back positions to the forward positions. Encourage them to dribble with speed down the line as they did through the coaching sticks in the last practice. Call out the record time so that each player can try to beat it.

Progression 2 – Following Figure 2-3 (Up-Back-Through: Progression 2), move one player from each corner queue to the cone gates simulating a mid-field player. At the of recreational soccer level, I consider it an achievement if you can simply get players to *not* let the ball roll by them. More often than not, there is a Defender waiting on the other side when they do. With an open body shape facing the field, have them receive with the inside of their furthest foot to control the ball. After taking control of the ball, have them quickly take the ball forward with the inside of their other foot. Emphasize that the pass to the player in the cone gate needs to be firm so that she can work with it. Weak passes give her less time to evade approaching Defenders.

There are many creative progressions and that can be added to this basic drill. If your team is a little more advanced, you might consider layering in some communications practice. Before passing to the player in the cone-gate, have the passer randomly call *"Turn!"* or *"Run!"* at same time she passes. If she calls *"Time!"*, the receiver should/can let the ball roll by her and turn and run onto it. The command to *"Turn!"* indicates that there is pressure behind and she should take a controlling touch during her turn. This simple nuance in communication can make the difference between gaining or losing competitive advantage.

This drill runs with two balls moving at the same time. Start balls on the two corners with players in the queue. Start the passing sequence in a counterclockwise direction. Corner players starts with a pass to the middle player and follow their pass. The middle player receives/passes to the corner player and then follows her pass. The corner player then passes to the player at the cone-gate and then follows her pass. The player at the cone-gate receives, turns, and dribbles to the far corner where she lays the ball off to her teammate and the sequence continues.

Up-Back-Through: Progression 2

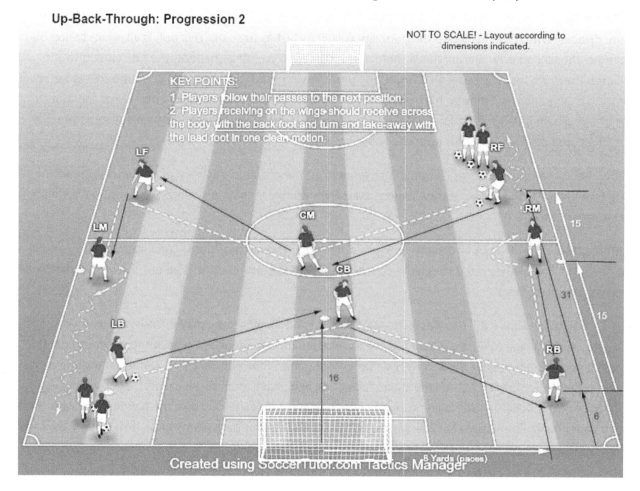

Figure 2-3

This drill involves a lot of running, so give your players periodic water breaks to help them stay hydrated and provide a little rest. Don't forget to change directions at appropriate times so your players can train their opposite foot.

Coaching points:

- Just like Rondo, encourage passing the ball across the body to keep passing options open. Tell them that passing behind the back 'kills the play' because their teammate must now turn toward their own goal to control the ball. Poor passing to a teammate in the middle can result in setting up the other team for a shot on goal...so be careful!
- Take at least one controlling touch before making the pass to the next player. If possible, make that controlling touch into space in the direction of the next player.
- Emphasize that everyone has a job, and if we do our job, the player on the ball knows where her teammates are so that she can get the ball to safety.

(25) L-Check Throw-In – Over the course of a game, your team will have the opportunity to throw the ball into play approximately 30-40 times. If the teams are equally matched, the probability of retaining possession is often about 50%. If you are playing a team that has been taught to be unafraid of ball, and to mark and intercept, the probability of your team retaining possession can easily drop to 25%. This means that your team could have 7-10 fewer opportunities to take the ball to the opponent's goal and your opponent could have as many more to take the ball to yours. Every little thing that you can do to improve your possession on restarts, and not just throw-ins, denies your opponent opportunities to attack.

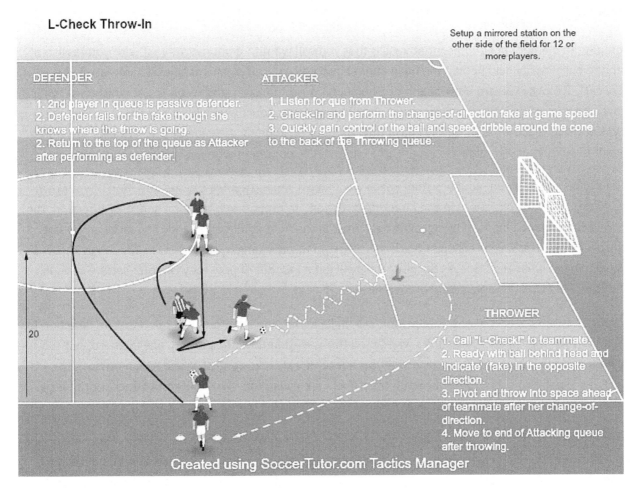

L-Check Throw-In

Setup a mirrored station on the other side of the field for 12 or more players.

DEFENDER

1. 2nd player in queue is passive defender.
2. Defender falls for the fake though she knows where the throw is going.
2. Return to the top of the queue as Attacker after performing as defender.

ATTACKER

1. Listen for que from Thrower.
2. Check-in and perform the change-of-direction fake at game speed!
3. Quickly gain control of the ball and speed dribble around the cone to the back of the Throwing queue.

THROWER

1. Call "L-Check!" to teammate.
2. Ready with ball behind head and 'indicate' (fake) in the opposite direction.
3. Pivot and throw into space ahead of teammate after her change-of-direction.
4. Move to end of Attacking queue after throwing.

Created using SoccerTutor.com Tactics Manager

Figure 2-4

At this age-level, everyone on your team likely knows how to properly perform a throw-in. If not, you may have to do some remedial instruction for players that are still struggling or are new. Otherwise, it's time to focus on some strategy to improve probability that your team retains possession during throw-ins. Up until this season, most of your players have probably been taught to 'throw it down the line.' There are better ways to increase your chances of keeping the ball.

This is a throw-in exercise that trains a few important skills at the same time by teaching your players how to: 1) Lose their 'Mark', 2) Play 'sneaky' soccer, and 3) Throwing into space ahead of their teammate. Losing a marking player is a skill that can be used all over the field, and fooling opponents to gain advantage is a mindset that you can't train too early.

With respect to layout, this is a simple drill to setup. See Figure 2-4 for the layout. Utilize the touchline to maintain a game-like feel for the training. Have a queue of 2-3 players at the touchline waiting to take their turn with the throws and a queue of 2-3 players at cones about 20 yards out from the touchline, one for defender and one for attackers.   20 yards is an effective amount of space to avoid congestion and support your players making their 'check in' runs to 'lose their mark.' If everyone is clustered around the thrower (i.e., within 10 yards), it is more difficult to execute tactics and retain possession. Training the thrower/receiver at this distance positions you to train broader team tactics later in your quest to improve possession.

If you have 12-15 players on your roster, you should be able to split them in to two training stations with one on each side of the field.

This drill contains an element of counter-intuitiveness that you will want to demonstrate first with your assistant coach. With the ball already held behind the head and ready to throw, call your assistant by name by saying, *"Coach, L Check!"* This way you are both clear on the expectations of thrower and receiver. At which time, your assistant coach 'checks in' (bursting run) directly at you (90 degrees to touchline) with the marking defender in pursuit. If you want to make it more realistic, have the defender positioned goal-side of your attacker. As a side note, you want to train your own players to mark 'goal-side' of the opponent when defending a throw-in.

At the tail-end of his check-in run, your assistant coach will make a single-step feint in the direction of your own goal before quickly changing directions in the attacking direction. In preparation for this change-of-direction, the player throwing can enhance the fake by signaling her throw in the 'wrong' direction and then pivot at the last second to throw in the attacking direction. I teach this throw-in to my younger age groups as the 'Pivot Throw-In'. This is the beginning of what I call 'Sneaky Soccer'...they will get a kick out of how they can orchestrate so much movement on the field with a simple swivel of their hips!

As soon as your assistant coach makes this feint, you will make a 'measured' throw-in in the opposite direction for him/her to run on. By 'measured', you want a well-timed throw-in that is on the ground, not too hard, not too soft, and just far enough ahead of the receiver's feet for her to quickly take control of and retain possession. Quick control of the ball and subsequent speed on the dribble are called for. Make sure the attacker dribbles as quickly as she can to the target cone and back to the end of the throwing queue.

The thrower then goes to the back of the Attacking queue, the Attacker moves to the back of the Throwing queue. The second Attacker in the queue will always function as the passive defender. In being passive, the defender should follow the fake, even though she knows which direction the ball is ultimately going to be thrown. It is her job to help train her teammate and give her a good sense of losing her mark.

IMPORTANT NOTE REGARDING THROW-INS: As a general rule, train your team that all throw-ins should be taken as quickly as possible. If you are in the attacking third, this *could* even mean that your Striker actually takes the throw if the ball is more convenient to her. This is to take advantage of the other team not being organized defensively. The faster you can take the throw, the less time you give your opponent to mark your own players. If for some reason the game is slowed down, such as the ball going far enough out of bounds that it takes more than 5-10 seconds to retrieve it, organize for this throw-in strategy.

Shooting Progression: After 15 minutes, turn this into a crossing and shooting drill.

L-Check Throw-In With Shooting

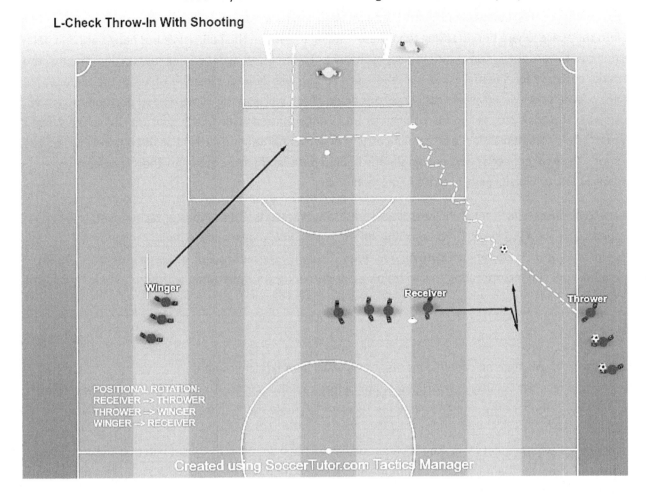

Figure 2-5

To keep the rotations simple, run this progression without a defender on the Receiver's back. Set your field according to Figure 2-5.   Replace the tall cone (or coaching stick) that the attacker was previously dribbling around with a low-profile cone. This cone should be in-line with the Thrower and the near post and approximately 9 paces out from the end-line. Add another cone (or coaching stick) on the far side of the field, even with the starting position of the receiver and about 5 yards in from the touchline. This will be the starting position for the Winger.

Run the sequence:

1. Thrower signals *"L Check!"* to the intended receiver. With ball behind head, Thrower fakes (indicates) in opposite direction.
2. Receiver sprints in, checks-away, then changes direction toward the opponent's near post.
3. Winger starts her run when the throw is made.
4. Winger calls for the "Cross!" when she and the Receiver meet pressure (the cone) in the goal area.
5. Winger take 1-touch shot into the net.
6. Rotation: Receiver → Thrower → Winger → Receiver

This drill trains timing of the supporting run. Instruct your Winger to *not* make her run too early and draw defenders into the space where her attacking teammate is going to receive the ball. Have her hang back and delay her supporting run toward the far post until the ball is thrown. This helps to avoid pulling marking-opponents into the penalty area early. When she makes her run, there will be one less defender in front of her in this already congested area. When the two attackers converge, this angle of run will give the Winger good position to receive a short pass across the goal face. When the ball-carrier and Winger have arrived in the goal area, have the Winger call out "*Cross!*". This communication lets the ball-carrier know that her teammate is in position to receive a pass and take a shot. The winger needs to be pacing slightly behind her teammate so that she doesn't receive an awkward square pass, or worse, a cut-back that goes behind her.

For your team to be successful in retaining possession on throw-in restarts, these types of tactics need to be practiced repeatedly. John Pranjic of 3-4-3 Coaching states, *"Over time, players will begin to recognize the movements and cues of their teammates both on and off of the ball in these throw-in situations."* (Pranjic, 2020) With this in-mind, consider incorporating this as training option during your pre-game warm-up to help ingrain the behavior.

Coaching Points:

- Have players move at game-speed. This means no walking or lazy checking-in.
- Do have the receiver <u>assume a casual demeanor before rapidly checking-in</u> to the thrower. This will catch the marking defender off-guard and allow the receiver to create more space and time for receiving the ball.
- Many players are too quiet. You may have to encourage them to raise their voices so that their teammates can hear them. This is a common-thread in communication throughout the entire season and requires constant encouragement.
- Warn your players ahead of time to not throw directly to an opponent. You wonder how this can even happen, but it does...even at higher levels of club play. It's absolutely bewildering why/how it happens, but it does. Be vocal and start training against it on the front-end of your season.
- Instruct your thrower to *'Get back into the game!'*. It's amazing how many players simply stop on the outside of the touchline after they have made their throw and simply watch play continue as if they have done their part and handed-off the ball. Get them into the mindset of sprinting to support their teammates after they throw.

(15) 4v4 Winner Stays On - This is a continuous and unstructured Small-Sided Game (SSG) that will help your players start to build endurance for their first game next week.

Following Figure 2-6, layout a field approximately 30 x 20 yards and evenly space two Pugg-style mini-goals on each end. This will encourage field switching and spacing amongst the teams. Split your players up into three teams of 4 with different colored pinnies. Don't worry if the teams don't divide evenly. If you have one or two extra players, just assign them to one of the groups based upon who you think needs a little more help (or not).

4v4 Winner Stays On

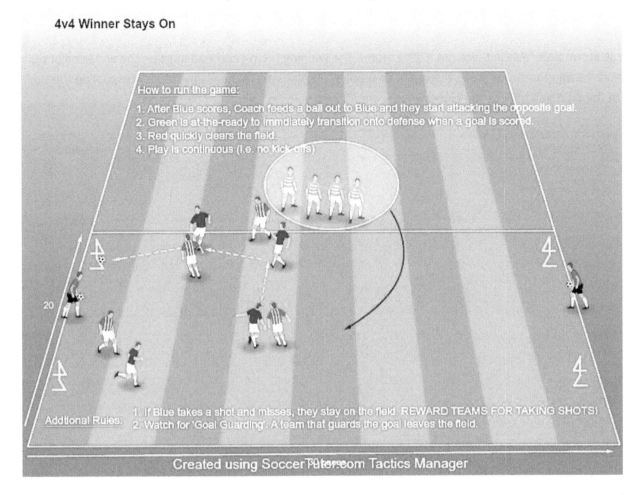

How to run the game:
1. After Blue scores, Coach feeds a ball out to Blue and they start attacking the opposite goal.
2. Green is at-the-ready to immdiately transition onto defense when a goal is scored.
3. Red quickly clears the field.
4. Play is continuous (i.e. no kick-offs)

Additional Rules:
1. If Blue takes a shot and misses, they stay on the field. REWARD TEAMS FOR TAKING SHOTS!
2. Watch for 'Goal Guarding'. A team that guards the goal leaves the field.

Created using SoccerPetereom Tactics Manager

Figure 2-6

Pick two teams to start. The inactive team is waiting on the sideline to immediately replace the team that is scored upon. The team that scores immediately plays the ball out of the net that they just scored in and the opposite goal becomes their attacking target. The team in possession does not wait for the team coming onto the field to start their attack as the game is continuous. If the team transitioning onto the field is not fast enough to prevent the team in possession from scoring, they leave the field. Emphasize that the team waiting to enter the game needs to be ready to transition quickly!

If you want to increase the pace of the game, have a coach positioned between each set of goals to quickly serve-in a new ball to the team that just scored. This will save them a few extra seconds retrieving the ball out of the mini-goal and keep maximum pressure on the team transitioning into defense.

Coaching Points:

- Encourage communication by having players calling for the ball.
- Encourage moving into space and 'stretching the field to support teammates and receive a pass.
- Encourage dribbling and the use of simple shoulder feints to fake defenders.

This drill can be tiring, so be ready to give them a little water break if needed.

(5) Run for Watermelon – Make them run a little more. The winning team gets head-start on the watermelon. Tell them that the biggest pieces are in the top of the cooler. Perhaps make them run around the goal on the other end of the field and back to the cooler.

Practice 2-2 - Email and Pre-Work:

Hey Parents,

Nice practice last night as the weather cooperated much better than was expected.

*'Thank You' to EK's Mom for tracking the number of 'ball touches' your girls made last night. She just tracked EK, but the count should be generally the same for all girls as they were executing the same moves during the same drills. The count was an awesome **877 touches over the course of our 1-1/2 hour practice!** I have heard the number '1000' thrown around as the number of touches required for practices to be transformative. Instinctively, I think 877 is higher than what most club teams train to and definitely higher than any recreational team.*

Last night we learned a valuable skill that your daughter can use to beat a defender, whether that defender is on her back trying to prevent a turn or directly in front of her. That move is the Step-Over fake. Last night we only practiced this in a static fashion to get the basic movement down. In the next couple of weeks, we will evolve this skill to turn the ball on a defender and when taking a defender straight-on. Here is a link that I would like you to have your daughter review and practice the move at home. This can be done in the living room as the ball doesn't even have to move at this point.

[Insert link to a video that you like]

We have far too many girls kneeling on the field and tying shoe strings that have come undone during practice. This is an event that we don't want happening during games. When your daughter's shoes come untied, they essentially take themselves out of the game for up to 20-30 seconds. This doesn't sound like much, but it's enough time for the competition to run by her and score a goal while she is addressing something that should never have happened. Here is a basically fool-proof method to tie your shoes that is only a small deviation from the standard method that most people use:

https://www.instructables.com/id/Worlds-Best-Shoe-Knot/

Also, please share with your daughters that we are going to have another chest-trapping contest Wednesday before practice.

Thanks,
Coach Scott

Practice 2-2: Chest traps, dribbling circuit, fake & finish, 4v4v4 SSG, and red light/green light

(-15) Chest Trap competition - Reference basic drill from Practice 1-2.

(15) Foot Skills - Setup a General Foot Skills Practice Area according to Figure 1-1. Have players align themselves between a set of cones to do their work.

(2) Tick-tocks - Reference basic drill from Practice 1-1.

(2) Flamingos - Reference basic drill from Practice 1-1.

(3) Outside/Outside/Inside Cut - Reference basic drill from Practice 1-2.

(3) Tight dribbling with pull-back turn - Straight dribbling cone-to-cone. Practice dribbling with the left foot, then the right, and then use both feet touching the ball with every step. Reinforce keeping the ball on the end of foot. The ball shouldn't get more than about 6 inches from the toe. Contact with the ball is more of a 'push' than a 'strike' in the forward direction. Make sure your players are turning their foot slightly inward and using outside area of their 'pinky toe' to move the ball forward. Don't worry about speed at this point, but rather focus on good form.

(3) Step-Overs (in-place) - Reference basic drill from Practice 2-1. No change from the previous session. Continue to focus on good form and speed of execution. Have players bouncing low and on the ball of their feet ready for you to signal the move.

(2) Step-Over competition: Have your players count how many step-overs they can do on a countdown from 10. A complete movement to each side of the ball constitutes a single step-over. A slow verbal countdown from 10 should yield a winner having executed somewhere in the neighborhood of 16 step-overs. If you have a tie between two or more participants, have a 'step-off' and double the time to 20 seconds. To charge the atmosphere a little bit, divide the rest of the team into two cheering camps; one for each competitor. The winner should end up doing about 29 step-overs for the championship; just a little bit lower than the split-time at 10 seconds...which seems normal for the additional time.

(2) Water break – Hot day...allow extra time for water and rest.

(15) Forward Fake Dribbling Circuit - Reference basic drill from Practice 1-2. Practice simple change of direction with inside of foot, single-lunge, and then double-lunge. Take the ball away with the outside of the foot with the lunge move. Coach (or coaches) should stand directly over the first cone to verbally assist the dribbler on which direction to initiate the fake in-order to take-away in the correct direction.

(15) Dribble the Coaches - Lunge Fakes – This is more of the same pre-practice warm-up from Session 2-1; lay the field out in the same manner. Coaches position themselves approximately 5 yards out from each goal post and serve two lines of dribblers starting approximately 10 yards out.

This activity continues to focus on timing and execution of the lunge fake. Ensure that your players dribble straight at the defender (You!) so that the defender has no way of knowing which direction any fake will occur. The ball should be close to their foot and they should be dribbling with the outside surface of the foot (think pinkie toe). A good rule for beginners is to dribble with the foot that is to the side of the direction they want to move. This gives them a slightly better angle of take-away on the ball to improve their chance of success. Ultimately, you want them comfortable executing in either direction.

For players that are having difficulty with the action, have them slow it down and guide them as they approach. Let them know that you are more concerned about proper execution of the skill than you are about speed while they are learning. Important to effective execution of this, and any other fake, is to not fake too early and to not fake too late. The move should be initiated at approximately 3-4 feet from the defender. Anything closer gives the defender room to get a foot on the ball; anything further away doesn't fool anyone.

If they mess up, don't let them go to the end of the line and have to wait another minute (or two) before they get to try again. Have them redo the skill immediately from a few yards out while the mistake and correction are fresh in their minds. In his book, Practice Perfect, author Doug Lemov encourages teachers of all persuasions to *"Try to shorten the feedback loop and achieve correction as quickly as possible after an action that requires intervention."* (Lemov, Woolway and Yezzi, 2012). This is one of many great pieces of advice that has made this book a 'go to' teaching reference for me.

(2) Water break – Hot day...allow extra time for water and rest.

(25) Gate Soccer – This game involves two teams of 4-6 players dribbling on multiple sets of coaching sticks (gates). There should be one more set of coaching sticks than the number of players on the team to ensure that there is always an open gate. For instance, if you have 5 players on a team, you will want to have 6 gates. At the U11 age level (roster = 12-13) you could probably have an equal number of gates as players on a team. If they figure out that they can position one player at each gate to block, you will have to adjust. This may mean creation of a 3rd team to rotate in, but hopefully it doesn't come to that. Having two team keeps everyone awesomely busy with you deciding when everyone gets a short break.

Set your field up according to Figure 2-7. You will need about one-third of the field to have enough space to lay the gates out. If you don't have coaching sticks, then just use cones. I like to use coaching sticks as they give a better target for play and it's clear when the ball does (or doesn't) pass through the gate.

Coaching Points:

- Play is continuous! Keep the energy-level high!
- Challenge for the ball as you would in a game. Use shoulders/arms when you can.
- Encourage teams to develop a marking strategy when out of possession.
- Losing team has to do 10 push-ups after each progression.
- Coaches keep extra balls handy to feed in as needed.
- Be vocal with your praise and encouragement.
- Encourage your players to be vocal in their support and praise of each other.

Intro and Progressions:

Progression 1 (6-8 minutes) – A point is awarded for each time a player dribbles through a gate. This is the easy progression. Encourage dribbling and passing to teammates. Players must be dribbling the ball through the gate and not passing the ball through the gate.

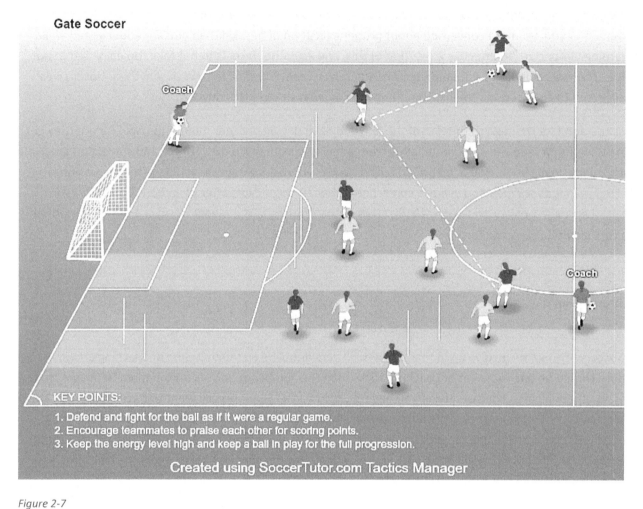

Figure 2-7

(2) Water break – Hot day...allow extra time for water and rest.

Progression 2 (6-8 minutes) – A point awarded for player making a pass through a gate to a supporting teammate on the other side. This progression encourages support for the player on the ball. Encourage players to spread out and not cluster around one or two gates on one end of the playing field. Encourage them to 'switch' the point of attack to teammates that are not marked or are nearer to open gates. Behaviors that you will observe are players slowing down or even stopping after they make a pass. Let them know they need to 'move' to continue supporting the teammate they just passed to.

(2) Water break – Hot day...allow extra time for water and rest.

Progression 3 (6-8 minutes) – A point is awarded for a player making a pass through a gate and that receiving player makes a connecting pass to another teammate. This drives even more support to score a point. Two teammates must then be combining with the dribbler to complete the passing requirement. Help the team in possession by calling out specific players to support the player on the ball. 'Support' is a common soccer term that it is good to get your players accustomed to hearing.

(2) Water break – Hot day...allow extra time for water and rest.

(10) Red Light/Green Light – This drill/game is meant to practice fast tight dribbling and turning from pressure in a fun way. In addition to simply being fun, this exercise forces your 'quiet ones' to raise their voices to call the game. This seems particularly important for girls. It seems that every roster I get, I have players that will not raise their voice for any reason. This takes patience, deliberate practice, and loads of encouragement, but you *can* get them to where they start to communicate on the field.

This drill is best played across the entire *length* of a field. If you don't have access to the entire field, just play across the width of the field in your own half. Start with all of your players evenly spaced on the goal/touch line (with a ball). They should be at least double-arms width apart so that they are not running on top of each other.

To start the game, the Coach positions him/herself on the opposite touchline and calls first round. When the Coach calls, "Green Light!", players tight-touch dribble as fast as they can toward the caller. When the Coach calls, "Red Light!", players execute a pull-back turn and the last player to stop with her foot on the ball goes back even with the last dribbler. Rather than having them go all the way back to the starting position, this penalty still gives them a fighting (albeit slim) chance to still win.

When each cycle is over, have the winner hustle back to the other side to call the next round. Consider investing in (or borrowing) a low-cost megaphone for the caller to use. You would be surprised at how many people actually have these laying around. Your players will absolutely love the novelty of it and it becomes a big part of the 'reward' for winning each round. Don't let previous winners call a second time so that you can spread the incentive around to the rest of your players.

Bending the rules: On some occasions, and to the playful groans of their teammates, I have given some incorrigibly slow players a head-start on the game. I yell encouragement to these players to, *"Don't blow this great lead!"*

Red Light, Green Light

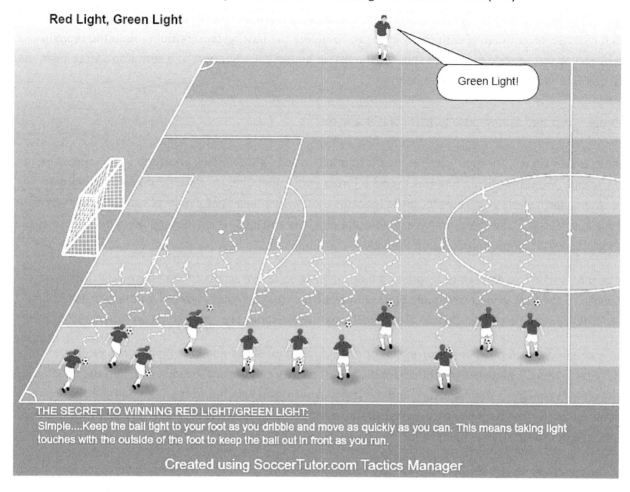

Figure 2-8: Red Light/Green Light

This drill surreptitiously helps your players improve dribbling skills and gain endurance as they are having fun!

After Practice – Pass out watermelon and distribute uniforms (if available).

Practice 3-1 - Email and Pre-Work:

Hi Parents,

Please share this email with your daughters.

We worked the girls hard last night so they weren't exaggerating when they got in the car and said they were exhausted. This is a high-energy group of girls and their hard work is going to pay off handsomely when their competitors start to shut-down in the second half of their games.

We have only been working on the step-over move for two practices and the girls are picking up on it fast! We saw VP, who is playing up a whole age level by-the-way, attempt this move during our small-sided game toward the latter part of practice. She didn't pull it off, but we could be no less thrilled given that she was bold and even attempted it after having only practiced it for a week. Please have your daughters to continue practicing this useful move between now and next practice. Also, please let them know that Coach [Name] and I want them to take these risks and try these moves in games. This is the only way they will become effective with these fakes and beat defenders. We will never be upset if they fail in their attempts; the important thing is that they tried!

Here is the link again for the tutorial for the Step-Over move:

[insert a link you like here]

Coach [Name] and I are also excited at how aggressively the team is playing. They have obviously retained a great deal of the training and mindset that we instructed in the Spring. We do have a 'watch-out' that you can help share so that we don't get penalized in games. When challenging for the ball on the run, it's OK to use shoulders, but NOT OK to raise the elbow (chicken wings) to push the opponent off the ball. Particularly important is to NOT raise the elbows in the penalty area (18-yard box) and have a foul called on us.

That's if for now. Keep them practicing over the next few days and we'll see you on Monday.

Thanks,
Coach Scott

Practice 3-1: 4v1 Rondo, foot skills, up-back-through, 6v6 unstructured SSG

(-15) Chest trap competition – *"Let's see who can knock [last winner] off of the championship throne."*

(10) 4v1 Rondo – Most soccer players of this age know this game as 'Monkey in the Middle' or 'Piggy in the Middle." We are going to rechristen it 'Rondo' as this high-benefit drill is commonly referred to in club and professional soccer communities. Rondo is hailed by many soccer professionals as one of the ultimate training tools to create game-like conditions to improve first-touch, passing, and decision-making skills.

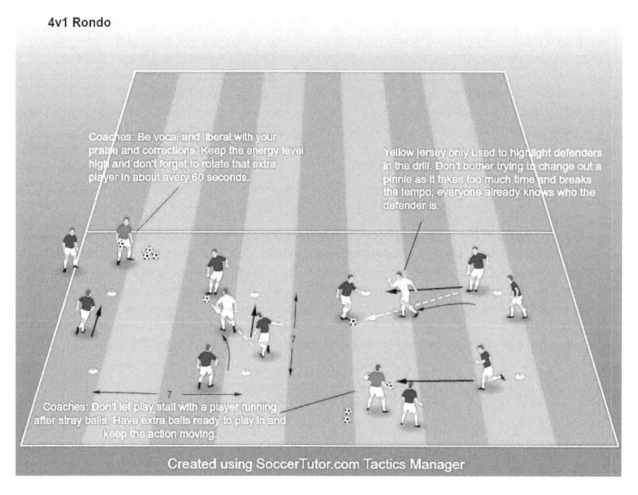

Figure 3-1

Rondo can have many different variations regarding the number of attackers, number of defenders, constraints on play, and other training objectives. This Rondo will be a simple 4v1 possession drill to start getting players conditioned to tight ball control and the elevated pace that we want them to play at.

Perhaps the most important aspect of administrating rondos is to keep the expectations and energy level as high as you can. I have seen many club coaches instruct their players to *"make a rondo"* and then leave it on auto-pilot. The consequence is typically that players will relax, make weak passes, decide whether or not they want to expend any energy trying to 'shag' an imperfect pass from their teammate, walk to fetch a stray ball rather than run, and argue about who should go in the middle. This is not the essence of Rondo and represents a failure on your part as a coach if you allow it to happen. If this happens, you are training sloth and not excellence. This doesn't just happen at younger ages; it will occur with older players too if you let it. It is for this reason that you want an assistant coach (i.e., authority figure) managing each Rondo. As a recreational coach, you will already have one assistant to help. Reach out to other parents for that additional help...there is often at least one parent with soccer experience just waiting to be asked!

For the setup, If you have a roster of only 12-13 players, you will only be able to have two active rondos and will have to substitute players in. As seen in Figure 3-1, layout 2 adjacent squares with sides of 7 adult paces. These squares should be at least 5 adult paces apart so that you don't have players on adjacent sides running on top of each other. In fact, they don't even need to be lined up with each other; just have them in close enough proximity to each other to take advantage of the communication and energy happening in both stations. Players in one grid will also hear the coaching points given in another. Though the sides of the Rondo should be about 7 paces in length, this is not a hard/fast rule. If you find that your players' skill level is such that they need more time to control the ball, increase the sides to 8 or 9 paces in length. As a rule, the tighter the grid, the faster and more unforgiving the action.

Restrictions/guidance for running the drill:

The primary restriction for this introduction is that players can only pass to a teammate to their left or their right and *not* across the grid. If they pass across the grid, they get to go in the middle. This means they can immediately return a pass to a player that just passed to them, or, pass to their teammate on the opposite side. Multiple touches are allowed as they get a feel for the drill. Make sure players on the outside don't 'drift' inward toward the defender. If they do, point out how they are taking away their own flexibility to make a connecting pass by reducing the space available. If a player on the outside continues to drift inward, make her switch with the defender and tell her, "*If you want to be in the middle, I'm going to let you.*" Give the defender some latitude in coming out to attack the ball carrier. I always make the first pass 'free' as the defender is inclined to mark the ball carrier before the action even starts.

Coaching points:

- Speed of Play – Remember to keep the energy level high. Be animated in your encouragement of the defender to really go after the ball. It is the effort of the defender that drives the pace of the drill.
- Passing/Receiving across the body – Demonstrate beforehand how/why you want them to pass across the body of their teammate. Passing across their body gives them two subsequent passing options. Passing behind their body reduces those options to 1, thereby making it easier for the defender.
- Communication - Encourage the girls to call for the ball and use their teammate's name.
- Movement without the ball - This is essentially getting them to use the movement that was trained in the 4v0 session a week ago. After they pass, move closer to the player they passed to in order to make themselves available for a pass back.
- Responsibility to make a bad pass a good pass - Start making it clear that each player has a responsibility to turn any bad pass into a good pass during the drill. The general rule is to make your best effort to get a foot out and 'shag' the stray pass and keep possession. If you don't feel this effort has been made, make them go into the center and defend.

Managing a youth Rondo isn't rocket science and you will be pleasantly surprised at how quickly assisting parents (with little or no experience) will start mimicking your corrections in the adjacent Rondos.

Examples of things you should hear yourself saying to your players during Rondo:

"The first pass is free. Defender, start in the middle and let the ball carrier make her first pass before you pressure"

*"Nice touch [**name**], that's the way to control the ball!"*

*"Great effort defending [**name**], I like the pressure you are bringing on the ball carrier."*

*"Oooops! [**name**] in the middle for making a pass that no one could receive."*

*"Step it up [**name**], you will never win the ball with that level of pressure."*

*"[**name**], try to make those passes across the body."*

*"Great job ladies! That was about [**number**] of passes in row!"*

"Way to snag that ball, [name]! [name] really owes you for saving her terrible pass." (deliver jokingly)

Sometimes you won't have enough players for a square. When this happens, consider making your square a triangle!

(20) Foot/Dribbling Skills – Setup a General Foot Skills Practice Area according to Figure 1-1. Have players align themselves between a set of cones to do their work.

(3) Tick-Tocks – Reference basic drill from Practice 1-1. The progression for this practice is to introduce forward movement. Angle the feet out ever so slightly to achieve the forward motion and move the ball from cone to cone. Execute a pull-back turn when reaching the cone to start movement in opposite direction.

(5) Step-Over and take-away w/inside of foot - Up until now the focus has been on getting your players comfortable and competent with the basic action of the fake. In this drill your players will perform a step-over, pivot, and take the ball in the opposite direction with the inside of their foot. This is the first drill with the step-over that introduces movement of the ball after the fake.

Have your players perform this drill on your command so that you and your assistant coach can easily see who is struggling with the move and needs individual attention. If the issues preventing good execution are common to a lot of players, take a quick break to demonstrate the skill again. If it is one or two players having trouble, have your assistant coach work with those players individually to get them up to speed. Quickly reset the ball between the cones after practicing each take-away so that you can get as many reps in as possible.

Mistakes to watch for and correct:

- One very common mistake to watch for is the step-over leg not clearing the ball enough for the foot doing the take-away to do its work. To be clear, the player starts a few inches behind the ball and ends a few inches behind the ball before the take-away is executed.

- Another issue that you might see is a player performing a scissors move instead of a step-over. Research the difference between the two if you are not already familiar. If you see this happening, praise the skill for what it is, but show your player the difference between the two and have her start training the step-over.

- Some players will also start immediately taking the ball away with the outside of the foot rather than pivoting and using the inside of the opposite foot. Indicate that this is not an incorrect method of taking the ball away, but it's not the skill that we are training presently. Let them know that you will be working on taking the ball away with the outside of the foot in later practices.

(5) Side-to-Side dribble w/ partner shadowing - This drill is designed to start getting players accustomed to having a defender at their back and screening the ball while dribbling. Progressions of the drill will help them develop composure in evading defenders and screening (protecting) the ball.

As with all new skills, demonstrate with your assistant coach what it is that you expect them to do. Start in-between the two cones dribble side-to-side changing ball direction with the inside of the foot. The dribbler should always have her back to the defender and *not* turned fully in the direction of the dribble. They will have to turn slightly to change directions, but their orientation to the ball should be mostly perpendicular as they move. The ball should remain several inches in front of the dribbler and not outside shoulders width. This means that a tight level of control needs to be maintained in order to shield the ball from the defender. To be clear, this is NOT 'shielding' as the player is moving the ball. In shielding, the ball is relatively stationary as the player protects it until help arrives or until she can turn.

There are multiple options for which part of the foot to use in turning and dribbling in this drill, but for now, encourage dribbling with the inside of the foot when changing directions.

Have a teammate from the adjacent set of cones 'shadow' the dribbler but not try to steal the ball. Challenge the dribbler to see how many times she can change directions in 30 seconds while still using good form to screen the ball. Have the partner shadowing count how many times she changes directions. Switch places so the shadowing partner can practice. Ensure the dribbler is constantly 'checking' her shoulder to see where the Defender is and not just focusing on the ball. Have the defending partner focus like a 'laser' on the ball (rather than the player) to trigger her defensive change of direction. This serves a secondary goal of training good defensive behavior in following ball movement rather than misleading cues of the attacker's body.

(7) Side-to-Side dribble w/ step-over - This drill is a small progression that introduces the step-over during the dribble just practiced. Demonstrate the technique and indicate that, instead of taking the next touch with the inside of the foot, perform a step-over and take the ball away in the opposite direction with the outside of the nearest foot. Don't despair as you watch them struggle with this new movement. It is going to take them a few practices to develop good coordinated movement but it will come. Be patient and continue to deliver as many positive corrections as you can squeeze into the time you have.

(3) Water break

(20) Up-Back-Through - Reference basic drill from Practice 2-1.

(30) 6v6 SSG (Small Sided Game) Unstructured - If you have access to a full field for training, pull one of the goals to the mid-field line for half-field play (preferred). If you don't have two large goals to play against, play across the width of the field with two Pugg-style mini-goals on either side. Make sure you have good separation between the mini-goals to encourage field switching.

You can play with or without Goal Keepers. If you play *without* Goal Keepers, which is more likely if you are playing with mini-goals, emphasize that, *"everyone attacks and everyone defends."* Ideally, you want to keep play unstructured at this point to see who is hungry for goals and which players have a tendency to lay back and play more defensive and supporting roles. This is especially important if there are many new players on your roster and you are still learning their personalities.

If your players are tending to bunch up, rather than making space and passing to each other, consider assigning specific defensive and attacking positions to establish boundaries. You can even layout 3 'swim lanes' to serve as boundaries to drive separation if necessary. If you do assign positions, rotate the offense with the defense periodically to give all players some opportunities to take shots on goal. If you are playing with Goal Keepers (preferred), it's a great time to start getting the players you expect to be in this position some time fielding shots.

When one team scores, simply have the other team play out of the back rather than restarting the game with a kick-off. If you are playing with GKs, have them yell *"Stretch!"* to get their teammates spreading the field in anticipation of a distribution from the GK. As you are playing on a short field, the GK should quickly distribute the ball in an underarm fashion to one of her teammates. If you are playing on mini-goals, simply have the closest player retrieve the ball and dribble out to restart play.

Throw some popular music on a portable speaker or boom box if you have one!

(10) Popsicles and/or ice towels – You can really make training enjoyable by the little things you do for your players. This part of the season can still be hot depending upon where you live. So, on days that hit 90 degrees or more, I will bring a small cooler of white hand-towels soaking in ice for them to refresh themselves with. These are always well-received and the parents will appreciate you looking after their kids in this way. You will find that many parents want to help and are often happy to take on this responsibility if you only ask them to.

Practice 3-2: Rondo, ABC defending, build-out Part-2, danger zone, and dominant player strategy

Make sure this practice hits just before your first game. This is important because it represents that last opportunity you will have to drill a few important concepts before your players compete and you want it to be as fresh in their minds as possible. This could be a tight schedule unless you start on time. Encourage your GKs to show up as early as they can to receive a little extra instruction.

(-30) For GKs - Practice punts for players expected to play GK in the first game. Your first choice should be to build out of the back, but impress upon your GKs to punish opponents with a punt when they all drop back to mark players in the defending third. DON'T BECOME PREDICTABLE! I've seen clubs that 'require' their youth teams to build out of the back without being given an option to punt, which, I believe, doesn't train the correct mind-set. Soccer is a game of deception and allowing your team to punt or play-out trains this mentality from the beginning.

Getting off a good punt to the Mid-fielders or Forwards can be challenging. The biggest problem hamstringing punt effectiveness is that most inexperienced GKs focus on kicking 'high' rather than far. Sure, they want to kick it to the other end of the field, but their desire to kick it 'to the moon' is not the right approach. The only thing that a high punt that doesn't clear the defending third does is give your competitor a chance to get to it before it hits the ground. Then, it's 50/50 defensive chaos all over again for your team. Begin instructing proper punt form as soon as you can.

There are resources online, but you are going to find that they are 'all over the board' with respect to technique. Not all are going to be appropriate for the level of coordination of your developing athletes. It's good to seek out several of these examples for best practices. When I was teaching my younger daughter to punt, here are the learning that I found most useful:

Teach them to hold and release the ball with one hand. It should be the hand opposite of the foot they will punt with. Many kids will want to use both hands to hold and release, but this hamper long-term style of rotating the hips into the punt for developing power.

The ball should be held as low as possible without affecting the run-up to the punt. By low, I mean around mid-thigh if possible. There are multiple benefits to keeping the ball low and releasing it low. For starters, a ball that is released at mid-thigh level will drop to at-least knee-level before it is struck with the instep. This places the ball much closer to the most power point in the leg swing and makes it more difficult to create 'pop flies' in the defending third. This technique produces lower-trajectory ball flight, that, if allowed to bounce once or twice, can easily end-up in the opponents defending third in short order. Fast, low-flying punts also prevent many opponents from converging on the ball quickly.

As for coaching points, be on the lookout for players that toss the ball into the air (shoulder level sometimes) and try to strike it as it comes down. This self-service is much more difficult to strike and the trajectory is often shanked left or right out of play, or worse, straight to a competitor.

Have your players practicing this technique start by punting into the net of a large goal. This will greatly increase the number of repetitions they can get off during the few precious practice minutes you have. Start with one-step into the punt until they get comfortable with the release and strike. After they gain some comfort, introduce a three-step run-up to the release/strike to help improve their power.

Once they gain some confidence after punting into the net, put them near the top of the 18-yard box as if they were actually punting. This gives them a better feel for how to judge their run-up to the line and not make the mistake of stepping over. Keep them fed with plenty of balls to practice their punts. You may have to steal a player or two from the small-sided games that are going on to help shag balls. Keep at least one coach near the players punting to give them timely corrections.

(-30) For everyone else – Setup two small fields and let them play 'pick-up style' games until practice starts. Lay pinnies out for them to put on as they show up to practice.

(10) 4v1 Rondo – See basic drill from Practice 3-1. Though your players should already be 'warmed up', you want to ensure that they get a significant number of quality touches on the ball during your practice. Rondo is one of the best tools for this objective. Keep everything moving and demand high-energy during this activity.

(40) A-B-C Defending – This is a refresher (from Spring) in organized defending. It includes static close-downs to reinforce cooperative defending technique and is followed by live 2v3 play. If you followed this curriculum in the Spring season, most of your players will remember the A-B-C defending tactics instructed. Though traditionally known as *Pressure-Cover-Balance*, we will refer to the elements as "A-B-C" where A=Attack (the ball carrier), B=Backup (back up the first defender), and C=Cover (the goal). The acronym "A-B-C" is simply easier for a 9-11 year old to remember. For those that weren't with you the previous season, you will have to pull them along in an OJT (On-the-Job Training) fashion.

Preparations: You should already have your line-up ready for your first game and have an idea of who will be playing defensive positions and who will be in the forward attacking roles. While the 'static' portion of this training will apply to everyone, the 'live' portion becomes 'functional' training where you want to organize your players by the positions you expect them to play in the first game.

Using Figure 3-2 as a guide, set out 3 mannequins serving as attackers about 18 yards out from the Goal line. Make sure they are evenly spaced with about 8 yards (big steps) apart. Place a ball at the foot of each mannequin to simulate an attacking figure. If you don't have mannequins, cones with balls on top of them will suffice. For each of the three mock-attackers, place a small-profile cone 5 yards off the Goal line and in-line with each mock Attacker. These small-profile cones will serve as queuing points for each wave of defenders practicing the cooperative close-downs. Identify the mock attackers from left-to-right as #1, #2, and #3 to your players.

(20) Static Close-Downs - Each cone gate will have 3-4 players in it and the players in the front will function as a backline that cooperatively closes down the attackers. If you are a stickler for detail like I am, organize your defenders such that they will be in the exact positions you expect them to play in the first game. This isn't always possible, given how many players you have and how they will rotate through the drill, but details matter. If you can give them a little early familiarity with who they will be supporting, it's all for the better.

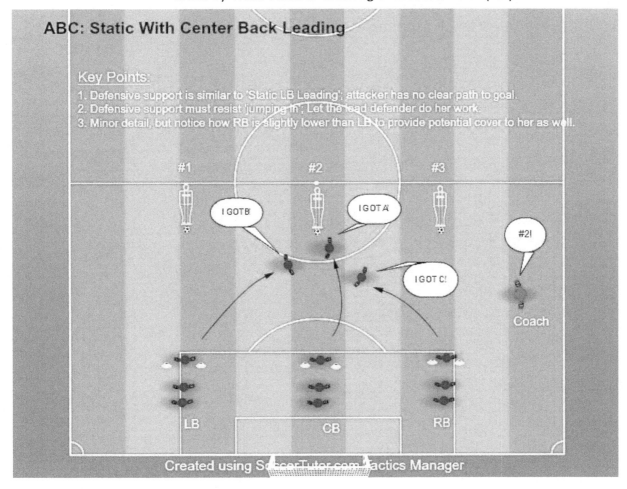

Figure 3-2: ABC Static With CB Leading

Running the static close-downs portion of this drill:

The coach calls out a number and the active group closes down cooperatively. The defender corresponding to the called attacker leads the close-down and yells, *"I got A!"*. Her adjacent teammate(s) will close down in support and yell, *"I got B!"*. If the 1st defender is on one of the wings, the 3rd defender will support the 2nd defender and yell, *"I got C!"*. The objective of the 2nd and 3rd defenders is to close the gaps where the attacker may be inclined to dribble or pass through. This makes positioning of the supporting defenders critical. They must not be too close or too far from the 1st defender. If they are too close, the attacker will dribble around them both. If they are too far, the attacker will simply dribble between them. I have found that a supporting distance of 8-9' between defenders does a good job of cutting down passing angles and thwarting all but the very best of attackers at this level.

The 'ABC Static' figures LB, CB, and RB respectively show close-downs for these positions. Though the graphics are a bit repetitive, there are different 'Key Points' on each that are worth noting. Ensure that players observe proper body shape closing down in each part of the field.

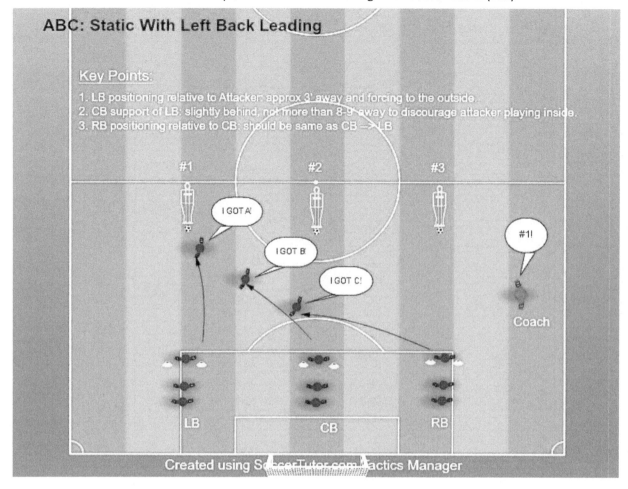

Figure 3-3: ABC Static With LB Leading

You want to give players as much practice as possible, so after a few random close-downs for each group, have them hustle to the ends of the lines. If you don't keep things moving, this amount queuing can result in your players becoming chatty and not paying attention. Tell them that they need to be paying attention to the corrections you are giving all players so that they don't make the same mistakes themselves.

These rotations should happen very quickly, including corrections. Send each group to the back of the line and run the next group. Do this for about 10 minutes.

Coaching Points:

- *Rule #1* – The 'A' defender always pushes the attacker toward the outside of the field.
- *Correct positioning* - There is so much that can go wrong with respect to close-down positioning and body angles. Correct these errors immediately and don't let your players proceed without doing so. If you have to physically position/turn a player to the correct angle, then do so.
- *Be vocal* - Encourage your players to remind each other who has the 'A' role and for themselves to call their supporting roles. Communication needs to be demanded and encouraged.

- *Be on your toes* – Players should not be flat footed after closing down, but rather on the balls of their feet ready to respond to the movement of the attacker.

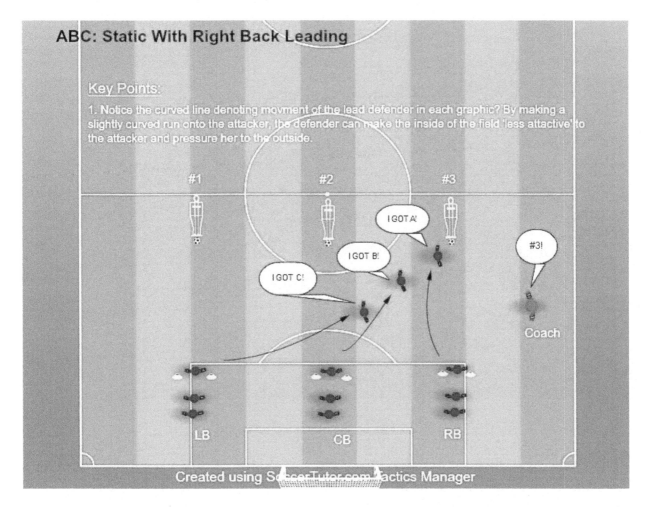

Figure 3-4: ABC Static With RB Leading

Progression 1: Now, let each 'wave' of defenders dynamically respond to a second and third random call to close-down. Randomly call one of the other attackers and have them adjust to each other as seen in Figure 3-5. This essentially represents the attacker 'switching' the point-of-attack with a pass to a supporting player. Do this a couple of times for each wave of defenders and try not to spend more than 10 minutes total for this progression before moving to live close-downs.

Try to position defenders in their planned roles in the lineup that you expect to use. For instance, if you have a player that you know will be playing Center Back, don't run her in one of the outside positions during this drill.

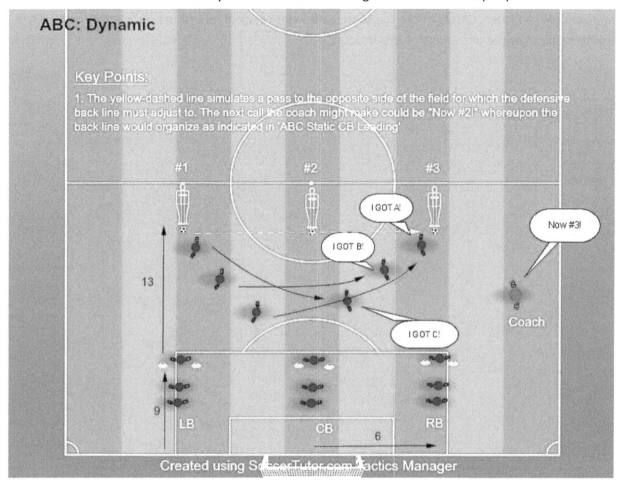

Figure 3-5

(20) Live Close-Downs: As the objective of this exercise is to improve defensive tactics, you will want to 'overload' the competition in favor of the defenders. This means that you will want only two attackers running at three defenders. This will make the drill less chaotic, improve the defenders' chances of success, and build their confidence in working together.

Using Figure 3-6, adjust the field to support the live close-downs. If you are using mannequins, pick them up and place two small-profile cone-gates at the appropriate distance for the attackers to start from. You might be sharing a field with another team, so lay the cones just short of the mid-field line so that you don't encroach on another team's space. This separation gives both attackers and defenders plenty of time organize their actions.

Divide your team appropriately into groups of attackers and defenders. Drill stations rarely work out perfectly. You'll probably have 13 players, so it's a great time to rotate your intended Goal Keepers in-between the posts so that they can field some shots that may get through. This is also a great opportunity to start training your GKs to communicate with their defenders. For starters, have your GK push the 'A' defender to start the close-down as soon as she recognizes the point of attack. Just a simple assertive command of, *"Jill, that's you! Close that attacker!"* or *"Jill, get tighter to Sarah and close that gap!"* or *"Push her to the outside! Don't let her in the middle!"* or *"Challenge, Jill! Sarah has your back!"*. The GK's can also deliver praise to their defenders to confirm good support of each other. Let everyone know that this is actually the job of a good Goal Keeper and that it's not to be interpreted as being bossy. Most 10-11 year old girls are already going to be a bit shy and disinclined to be vocal for fear of being labeled. You've got to work hard to overcome this belief and help them understand that the team that communicates best with each other has the greater chance of success. If your assistant coach has some experience in the game, it would be a great time to have him/her behind the GKs during this exercise for the purpose of prompting this communication.

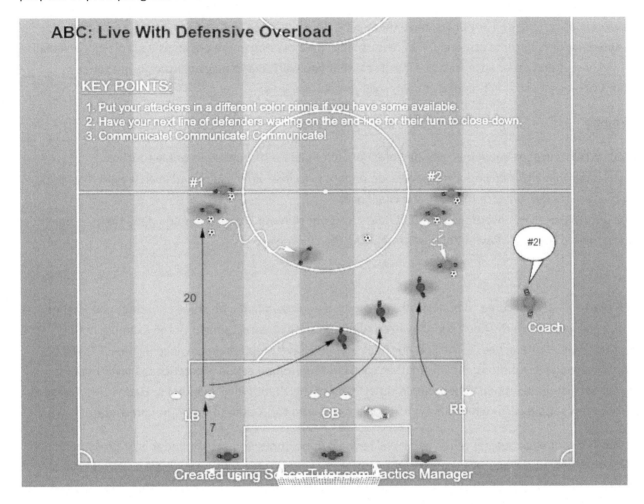

Figure 3-6

If you have time, switch groups so that each gets a chance to practice attacking and defending, but you want to start them according to their intended role so they have the benefit of calling the names of players that they will most likely be supporting at game-time.

Run the drill: Position 3 of your defenders on their cones with the next wave back on the end-line waiting. Position two attackers in a queue at each cone and each with a ball. Identify the attackers from left-to-right as #1 and #2 as you did previously. Explain that only two attackers will come out and the number that is called will be the one that plays the ball out; the other attacker leaves her ball behind.

As soon as the number is called, the defense should spring into action using the skills that have just been trained. Play ends when either the defense clears the ball or the attackers get a shot off. Some attackers will try to cheat and take shots from distance. You don't want to completely discourage this, but for this drill, they need to dribble into the 18-yard box. Tell them they can take their shot anytime they get inside the 18.

Attackers go to the backs of their lines and defenders to the backs of theirs. Keep cycles of play moving as quickly as you can. As soon as a cycle of play ends, start the next group immediately. Don't let attackers walk back up through the middle of the field when they are finished; make them hustle off to the sides and back up to their queue. If you pay attention to time-management, you can get many more cycles of the drill in...which translates to more skill building.

After each group has run the drill 3-4 times, have them get a drink and then switch roles; attackers become defenders and defenders become attackers. There is usually some overlap in the positions your players will play. Because of sicknesses and other absences, it is inevitable that you will have to play an attacking player as a defender (and vice-versa), so don't neglect training everyone in this area.

Coaching Points:

- Focus on closing gaps between covering defenders to eliminate through balls or big touches.
- Focus on proper close-down form (speed, side-on, not too close, knees bent and even weight distribution on the feet, jockey, wait for mistake, and challenge).
- As a principle of play, encourage your defenders to sprint to meet the attacker and deny them as much space toward the goal. Beware of overcommitting the closedown.

(40) Stretch (Part 2) – It's now time to practice breaking out of your own half with some choreographed action. At this point, you should have the line-up you want to run for your first game...similar to the example in this section entitled "Build-Out Practice." The line-up sheet that you have prepared in advance (Figure 3-7) will be used to manage the player rotations and ensure that each choreographed action is practiced. Player pre-positioning for each choreographed action should reflect that of the 'Out of Play' diagram in Figure 1-6. The goal keeper distributions should occur while players are accelerating into the 'Catch them Unprepared' state.

The players and GKs for each quarter of the game will have an opportunity to practice under light pressure in the positions that they will be playing. The players not practicing positional play will offer pressure. If you have a roster of more than 13 players, make sure the number of opponents pressuring is not more than four; It's going to be tough enough in the first game, so you want them to get a feel for a successful build-out. These four (or even fewer) players, however, should be going all-out to pressure the ball and spoil the play.

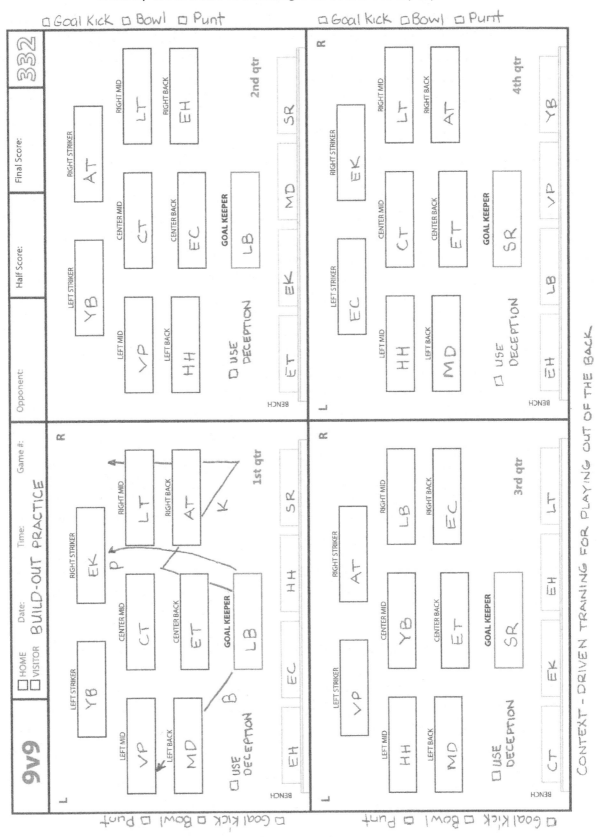

Figure 3-7

(Budget 10 min. for each quarter's lineup; you will have to move quickly to meet this goal.)

With the participants of the 1st quarter, start by having them assume their positions in the correct attacking shape...just as if the GK yelled *"Stretch!"* and they reached the spot where they are supposed to run to. Make the point that when the team in possession is spread as wide as they possibly can, it is impossible for the other team to effectively cover everyone. Generally, the opponent will leave three defenders (along with the GK) on their side of the half-way line during goal kicks or punts. This leaves 5 of their players to cover 8 of our players. Do the math! This means that 3 of our players will always be open. Even if they brought one more defender down, there will still be two players that they can't mark! This is the advantage that we want to exploit by getting REALLY wide and making marking difficult. Make this clear to your team by physically pointing this out.

For each quarter, the line-up and associated GK will get to simulate 3 different scenarios at least one time: 1) A distribution after collection, 2) A goal kick, and 3) A punt. The goal kick should NOT to be a lofted kick, but rather a heavily weighted pass on the ground to an open teammate. The distribution after collection should be a bowling-style delivery. Both of these distributions should be made to the highest possible teammates that offer the least amount of risk to possession. In other words, if you can distribute to a mid-fielder, do that before you automatically distribute out to the left or right back. Playing out-of-the-back doesn't mean you have to *always* play through the Outside Backs!

Though it's an aspect of the modern game, not too many youth coaches actually train starting their attack from the back; most prefer the safer long-ball strategy (punting). I have seen many coaches require their teams to ONLY play out of the back. While well intended, this really makes no sense. Once the competitor knows that your team isn't allowed to do otherwise, they will become comfortable drawing in close to tightly mark your players. This strategy then becomes counterproductive and even disadvantaging with the inevitable turnovers in your defending third. Instead, instruct your GK to make a judgement as to whether a punt or ground distribution is appropriate. When the competitor draws in close to mark-up and leaves your outlet Striker less guarded, tell her that that is the time to punt. When the opponent then chooses to cluster more in the middle of the field, tell her to play out comfortably to an outside back. The objective is to keep the opponent off-balance and this can't be done by being predictable. Keep them guessing!

The goal of every choreographed action in this session is to get the ball to the Outlet Striker (RF). For each scenario, put a stopwatch to the time it takes to get the ball to the Outlet Striker. This adds an element of pressure without actually adding additional defenders and creates an element of urgency.

As will be done in the game, ensure that that there are extra balls (approved by Refs) beside each post of the goal you are defending. These will support the very fast restart that you are looking to accomplish on goal kicks. PRO TIP: While the 'home' team is responsible for providing a game ball, the rules DO NOT prohibit you from bringing your own balls for use. Just make sure they are in good shape and inflated to 9-10 lbs of pressure. Every Referee that I've ever encountered hasn't had an issue with it, though sometimes they make me offer one up to the competition to put behind their goal.

Instruct that all goal kicks are to be taken in the middle of the 6-yard box. This improves unpredictability and makes is more difficult to mark your team when they are spread wide on the field in their attacking shape.

Pick 2-3 girls that want to play keeper. Have two of them perform the role of Defender and the other two will rotate in/out of goal during the exercise. You might want to add one more Defender on the field if possession is good. Pinnie the GKs in orange and the field players in blue.

Everyone needs to be prepared for a pass at any time. Reinforce presenting in the channels and the Outlet Striker's movement at mid-field.

Practice the 'Fast Goal Kick' by simulating the ball rolling out the end-line. This means, you as coach, take the ball and physically roll it out the end-line and announce a "*Goal Kick*". The starting point should be a deliberately staged cluster of players at the top of the 18 (see 'Out of Play' diagram in section 1-6.   This is a good representation of positioning at the time the ball rolls out of play. After you announce "*Goal Kick*", the GK (and everyone else) should yell, "*Stretch!*" and spring into action. It shouldn't take any longer to take the kick than it does for sprinting players to get into their attacking shape, which is 3-5 seconds. Ideally, the distribution should be made as the players are arriving into their target positions. Make sure that they are checking their shoulders to see if the Goal Keeper is targeting them to receive the ball.

Teach the Goal Keeper how to incorporate a little deception into her Goal Kicks and distributions. Show the Goal Keeper how to control and even fake the field. The Goal Keeper is like an orchestra conductor in the backfield...lots of power. Show her how to run over the ball (fake) and turn and pass in the opposite direction. Think Step-Over! These Goal kicks should be hard, straight, and on the ground. For GK collections, demonstrate the use of the underhanded distribution that flings the ball out far as possible to avoid frictional resistance of the grass. For punts, ensure your Keeper comes out to the edge the 18-yard box but doesn't go over.

Finally, get your defense in the habit of moving up the field to support the attack as the ball leaves your half.

Coaching Points: (too many to list, but focus on these few items)

- When playing out to the wide Mids and Backs, make sure the pass is a 'leading pass' into the space ahead of the player, otherwise you will pay dearly.
- *Everyone* yells "Stretch!" when the ball rolls out of play. It's not just the Goal Keepers responsibility to communicate.
- Use the balls stationed by the posts for fast restart Goal Kicks. During the game, make sure you assign responsibility to a player on the bench for keeping replacement balls at-the-ready.

When I first started coaching, I found and amazing resource offered by Brant Wojack, a high school coach out of Hawaii. The 9v9 Line-up Sheet (Wojack, 2020) utilized in this section can be found on his site and includes just about every variation of formation that you can think of. If you end up using one of Brant's templates, I would encourage you to 'buy him a beer' via a small PayPal donation. These sheets have been wonderful for my own organization and I find that my players like them too. All of my lineups are completed before the day of the game, so players can easily check to see what quarters and positions they will be playing. It saves a lot of "*Coach, when am I going in again?*" type of questions. In the beginning of the season, I will actually distribute the lineup to parents the day before the game. I do this so that, as the cheering section, they have an easy reference to every player's name. I have found this to be very well received. This is great at the recreational level as turnover on teams can be has high as 50-70%.

One last word regarding formation. This training curriculum focuses on the use of a 3-3-2 (3 defenders, 3 mid-fielders, and 2 attackers) formation for the season. If you are inexperienced and unfamiliar with the many considerations affecting selection of a formation, you can confidently use the 3-3-2 without agonizing about your decision. This is a balanced formation that won't leave you exposed on defense or weak in the attack.

(5) Emphasizing the DANGER ZONE - It's not safe to assume that your players *really* understand the urgency of clearing the ball when it finds its way into your goal area; especially when you have new players on your team, and more critically, when they will be defending.

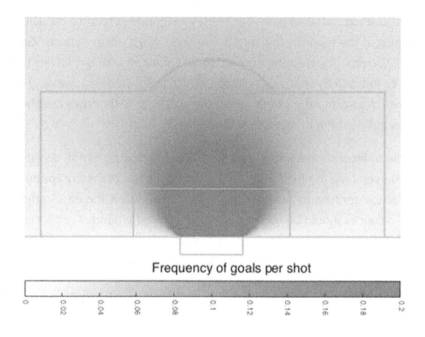

Frequency of goals per shot

Figure 3-8

In his book <u>Soccermatics</u>, mathematics professor and soccer enthusiast David Sumpter shares a heat-map (Sumpter, 2017) that illustrates the 'Frequency of goals per shot' when attackers take shots from different parts of the field. Of particular note is the tight oval area in red directly in front of the goal face. This is the 'DANGER ZONE' and you need to make a serious impression upon your players as to how this area needs to be defended.

You train your players to do their utmost in preventing the ball from getting this close to the goal, but inevitably, it will. Therefore, you need to create an 'Anything Goes!' mentality for clearing the ball from this area. Here are three simple rules for creating that mentality:

RULE #1: When engaging/defending in this area... **NO DRIBBLING!** This is not the time to try to control the ball and dribble out of the mob. You are not going to make it. With FEROCITY, clear the ball out to either side. When in this zone, clearing out to the side is preferable to down the middle as there are fewer opposing players on the sides that can pose a threat. If you do a weak clearance up the middle (which is more likely at this age of play), the likelihood of there being an attacker waiting for the ball is very high. A less preferred course of action, but preferable to clearing back up the middle, is to kick the ball out of play over the end-line if pressure is overwhelming at the outside post. This will force a corner, but at least gives your team time to organize defensively to meet the threat. Re-enforce to your players that you will not be upset if they have to do this; it's better than having to come from behind one more goal. This strategy might be controversial to some, so instruct it (or not) **as you see fit**. I wouldn't apply this strategy beyond this age-level as it becomes too risky. Beyond U-11, corner kicks are stronger and the threat of headers is starting to present itself.

RULE #2: **Use *any* part of your foot** to strike and clear the ball! These are 10-11 year-olds that have been drilled for their entire 'careers' to turn their foot 90 degrees and make a straight and properly weighted pass with the inside of their foot. This is going to be their mentality for clearances in this zone unless you update the context! The proper context in this case is that of an Emergency, where there is absolutely no extra time to optimize and choose which surface of the foot to use. Give every one of your players a license to use their TOE, outside of the foot, or even their heel to get the ball clear of the goal. Also, tell them you want them to use either foot to make the clearance regardless of how awkward it may feel. It doesn't have to be pretty; it just has to get the job done.

RULE #3: **DO NOT adjust on the ball** to use your dominant foot. This is a corollary to Rule #2. Don't get caught doing the "soccer dance" (demonstrate a ridiculous looking adjustment on the ball to align with the dominant foot) and leave time for an attacker to reach the ball. Remarkably, less than 1 second can determine whether or not you hear the other team cheering a goal.

COMMUNICATION: There is no more important time to communicate with your teammates than when the ball enters the penalty area. EVERYONE should be communicating, *"Turn it to the outside!"* or *"Clear it out the side!"* or *"Get it out of the middle!"* You are doing your teammates a disservice if you are not raising your voice and communicating this important information.

To demonstrate this, position several balls around the DANGER ZONE and physically demonstrate how you want them to clear the ball. Boot the ball out the side with your left toe, turn and boot the ball out the side with your right toe. Tell them to, *"Kick the crap out of the ball!"* to clear it. Then have them repeat it back to you as a team…they'll get a small charge out of having a license to yell the word crap.

(5) Dominant Player Strategy – This subject is less about field training and more about strategy for your first game. If you are a recreational coach, the Fall season seems to bring with it Club/Select players that, for one reason or another, aren't playing 'competitive' soccer anymore and find their way opposite your team on the pitch. At best (for you), they are washed-out players with only better-than-average skills. Worst case, they are really good players that can have upwards of 300 hours of training/game-time that will attack through your team like a hot-knife through butter. I believe the actions of fielding players like this in a recreational setting is ethically questionable, but it's not against any rules. You *must* be ready to defend against this caliber of player *before* the kick-off, otherwise you will likely pay for it immediately. This readiness includes clear communication to all of your players so they know what to expect and recognize it when it is happening.

In one anticipated game of the season preceding this book, my assistant coach and I observed a competitor's warm-up where a few players were demonstrating very strong dribbling and shooting skills. These high-level players will unwittingly showcase their skills for you. We were ready, especially after having had an extremely high-level player unleashed on us by the same club the previous Fall. Our strategy would be to 'man-mark' their two most capable players out of the game as best we could. When using this strategy, you are betting that the collective capabilities of the rest of your team are greater than the rest of theirs. Normally, you will only have to deal with 1-2 players of high caliber; in this game, we were having to deal with 3-4…a significant disadvantage. During the course of this game, the opposing coach begrudgingly admitted to fielding 4 former club players when pressed.

Here is how this will typically play out relative to 9v9 play. The dominant player will almost always line up at Center Mid (CM). This should serve as verification of your pre-game observations. The CM position is like being the Queen on a chess board for this player...she has more latitude-of-movement on the field than any other player. Good team-based soccer should reflect players that play and support appropriately from their positions. What you are likely to see, in this circumstance, is a player that goes everywhere on the field without restraint. These players will, without regard, often run over their own teammates to play the ball. For these reasons, you should be ready with your man-marking match-up at your own CM position. If your CM is not already your fastest and most aggressive ball-winner, then you need to adjust your lineup.

If your competitor is kicking-off first, your CM need to get on (and stay on) this dominant player as soon as the ball starts to roll. Chances are good that the starting pass will go to their dominant player. This means that your marking-player needs to apply effective pressure and work to not get beat (i.e., not rushing in and getting beat on the dribble). Your player should challenge if she gets a chance, but should be satisfied if the dominant player simply passes the ball off to a teammate. At this point, your player doing the marking should stay with the dominant player and resist chasing after the ball. Your player needs to follow her mark into all 4 corners of the field if that where she takes her. The job of your marking player is to ensure that their play-maker gets **no more action on the ball!**

If you don't cover a player with high capability on the kick-off, you could end up paying for it within a matter of seconds (literally). This marking process has to begin immediately. I tell my own players that they need to become her new best friend, never straying more than an arm's length from the mark! From their experience in club environments, these players are comfortable with the tussle and physicality of the game, so help your own players understand this and be ready to give/take the same in return.

This role of marking a dominant player can be demanding job for one player given the typical conditioning of competitive players. To account for this, make sure you have a backup ready to substitute-in to give her a break, essentially 'tag teaming' the mark. given that defenders don't typically run as much, you can also consider switching this player with one of your defenders to give her a break. Have your players coordinate with each other as to when they need a break. Have them make sure to not leave the mark exposed when they make the switch (i.e., make sure the mark is covered at all times).

The other coach will likely recognize what you are doing and make adjustments. He/she might try to pull their player from the game for a rest. When this happens, rest your own player so that she can be ready for when the dominant player is reintroduced to the game.

If you have two strong players to mark, you will have to determine from where to pull your 2nd marking defender. Remember, you don't need to use your most capable ball handler for this task, you need the next fast/aggressive player to help thwart possession. I generally play a 3-3-2 formation, so I assign my lesser capable Striker to the 2nd mark, thus leaving my defense intact and wingers to support our lone Forward. If you have at least one striker with good play-making abilities, you still have a chance of winning. Otherwise, you are realistically hoping for a tie as the best outcome.

Another critical aspect of being effective in attacking under this configuration is executing very fast restarts on goal kicks and punt distributions. With your Forward already alone at the top and heavily marked, it only gets worse if you allow the other team extra seconds to get back and get organized. IMPORTANT: If you have two dominant attackers in your third of the field while your team is learning to play out of the back, you are also more likely to get burned. For this reason, forget playing out of the back and seek to get the ball to the other end of the field as quickly as possible (i.e. Punt!).

Finally, being the player responsible for marking a dominant opponent is as psychologically challenging as it is physical. Your marking player has been given a clear responsibility and there will be times that she falls short and goals will be scored. Make it clear to everyone that the ball had to go through many other players for this to happen and that it is the entire team's responsibility to prevent goals. This can negatively impact your player's perception of herself if you don't qualify the expectations. In the presence of the entire team, your job is to offer her unconditional support and praise for the job she is doing. If the dominant player succeeds in scoring a goal, keep praising/encouraging your player by letting her know that she is making a difference. Don't miss any opportunities to proactively (and loudly) praise her defensive efforts when she shines.

Preparing for your team's first game

Preparation needs to start before the morning of your first match. Ideally, you will want to have your line-up finalized the day before so that you can share it with your players and parents. The benefit of doing this ahead of time, at least for the first couple of games, are two-fold:

1) It serves as a guide for the parents who, most likely, don't know the names of all the players on the team; It gives them a real name to be associated with the position on the field when they are cheering.

and

2) Every player knows her expected role ahead of time so that there is no confusion. In using a standardized format for the line-up, as seen in Section 3-2, you will also be creating a consistent structure in the communications process that your players will come to appreciate.

Soccer is a game where the team that communicates with each other the best will have some level of advantage over its competitor. But the advantage that you are working to create on the field shouldn't stop there. You can easily leverage the parents in your efforts to communicate and prepare your players. In addition to the line-up, you will want to share a list that contains just a couple of key responsibilities by position that your parents can share with their daughters. These responsibilities can easily be matched up with the player/position on the lineup. Though most parents of recreational soccer players don't fully understand the game, this is a simple task that they can confidently complete. Most are eager to do so, and by engaging them to help, you have provided them with a sense of contribution.

Enlist the Parents

The following content is what I include in the email with the scanned lineup as an attachment. Note that these are also great points for you to reinforce during the game as much as you are able to:

Subject line: Lineup and positional instructions for our 1st match

Hi Parents,

Attached is the lineup for our first match on Saturday. For those of you that are new, this will help you cheer for the players whose names you don't yet know.

In addition to this, here are a few position-specific pointers for the position(s) your daughter will be playing. Please share these so that, together, we can continue to reinforce what their responsibilities are:

Everyone:

- Communicate, Communicate, Communicate! Yell *"Stretch!"* on GK distributions.
- Fast restarts on everything! Goal Kicks, Throw-ins, and Free Kicks.

Goal Keeper (GK):

- All goal kicks taken from the center of the goal box. Be sneaky!
- Play out of the back if you can, punt when needed to keep them off-balance.

Left/Right Backs (LB, RB):

- You are primarily responsible for ALL throw-ins on your side of the field...unless there is a clear advantage of a forward player immediately taking the throw. Keep your feet on the ground and bring the ball all the way behind your head when making your throw.
- DO NOT dribble in the back field! Try to keep touches on the ball to just 1 or 2 as you pass the ball to your midfield teammates.

Center Back (CB):

- You are the boss of the back field. Make sure that the Left or Right Back is pushed forward when the play is in one of their attacking wing.
- Make sure that your back line is never 'flat'...meaning that all of the defenders are never playing even with each other to have all three beaten by a single through pass.

Left and Right Midfielders (LM, RM):

- Remember that your job is to attack *and* defend, so you will be running a lot.
- Use your speed to move the ball when you have open space in front of you. Think about dribbling through the slalom sticks like you did in the first week of practice.
- When we have 'Stretched' the field for Goal Keeper distributions, remember that you should be so wide on the field that your foot should actually be touching the white line!

Center Midfielder (CM):

- While you are expected to participate in the attacks, your job is primarily to setup the Strikers with through-balls (passes) that eliminate the defense. Take the big shots on goal when you have a chance, but also setup the Strikers to do their job in the front.
- If we identify a DOMINANT PLAYER on the field, your job is to mark her whenever she is on the field. This means being touch-tight on her wherever she moves in the defending half whether she has the ball or not. If she moves all the way down in the corner of the field, you stay with her and make sure she doesn't get the ball. The dominant player should never be unmarked.

Left Striker (LF):

- VERY IMPORTANT – When playing out of the back, remember that you drop down into our half of the field (even with the Center Midfielder) to draw the attention of their Midfield. If you are all the way back between the two defenders in their backfield, their Midfield Defender is free to mark one of your teammates, thus eliminating a passing option for your Goal Keeper.
- Watch your fellow striker during attacks to make sure she is not off-sides and call her back if necessary.

Right Striker (RF):

- VERY IMPORTANT – When playing out of the back, remember that you are the 'outlet player' for passes out of the back. The means you need to drop to just inside our side of the mid-field line and you are free to move to either side of the field tracking with the ball.

- Watch your fellow striker during attacks to make sure she is not off-sides and call her back on-sides if necessary.

Thanks,
Coach Scott

Treat pre-game warm-up as training

If you have 10 games over the course of your season, you have the opportunity to leverage another 5 hours of training with your team. If you only train 1 hour, twice per week, this translates to a whopping 25% increase in the time you get to train skills and give valuable correction! All too often, I have seen teams straggling late to the field and engage in aimless, low-energy activity that benefits no one.

Set the expectation with your team that everyone needs to be at the field at least 30 minutes early. Communicate your mindset with the parents so that they understand the importance of this 30 minutes.

Long-Passing

Not everyone will arrive to the field on-time, so as they arrive, you need to engage them in some productive activity to start warming up. As they arrive, have them find a partner and start long-passing with each other. By long passing, I mean anything longer than 20 yards. This non-descript activity isn't just meant to occupy your players as they arrive. It's a critical activity that helps to build leg strength with the objective of making long straight passes through defensive lines. I mostly see competitors passing casually at a distance of 7-10 yards. Train to the 'stretch goal' of a heavily weighted pass at 20 yards and then the 7-10 yard passes will become a 'no brainer.' Don't neglect to train the weaker foot! Let them start with their dominant foot and then call out, *"Switch to the opposite foot!"* after a short period.

Criss-Cross Finishing

After you have at least 8 players show up, you can begin a favorite warm-up I call 'Criss-Cross Finishing.' This warm-up trains first-touch ball control, shooting, and the concept of 'hunting for rebounds.' If an attacker remains static after taking her shot, she won't be in any position to take advantage of balls deflected back in her direction. Hunting for rebounds is the important habit of following-up a shot on goal in anticipation of the Goal Keeper mishandling the ball and creating another opportunity.

This is a warm-up that you should consider using before most games unless you have some other remedial training that you need to accomplish, so introduce it immediately. Normally, you will have enough time to conduct a couple different warmups, but as you are introducing this for the first time, plan on just doing Criss-Cross Finishing before your first game.

There isn't much in the way of preparation that you have to do to run this warm-up. Simply place two cone-gates approximately 20 yards out and about 12 yards wide of each post as represented in Figure 3-9. Evenly distribute your players between these two cone-gates and beside each post. You need at least 8 players to start this warm-up. Split the balls evenly between the players at the two posts; These players will be passers. If you have one (or two) Goal Keepers, this is a great time to get them some action, so let up to two at a time field shots. As the coach, you will be positioned inside the goal (behind the goal line) with a supply of balls.

Criss-Cross Finishing

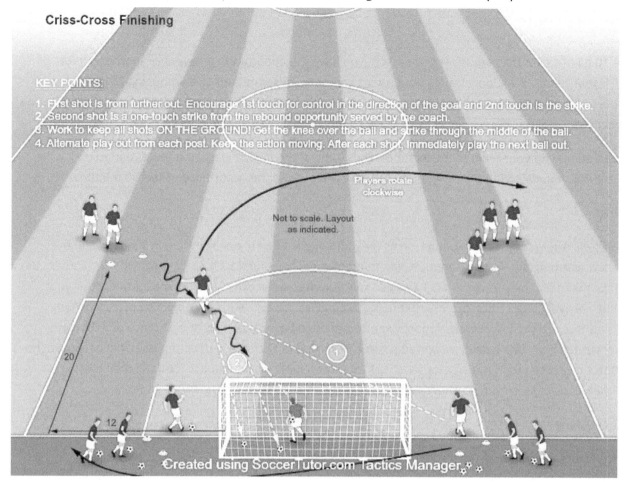

KEY POINTS:
1. First shot is from further out. Encourage 1st touch for control in the direction of the goal and 2nd touch is the strike.
2. Second shot is a one-touch strike from the rebound opportunity served by the coach.
3. Work to keep all shots ON THE GROUND! Get the knee over the ball and strike through the middle of the ball.
4. Alternate play out from each post. Keep the action moving. After each shot, immediately play the next ball out.

Figure 3-9

A player at either post can start the sequence by making a heavily weighted (hard) pass on the ground to the player waiting at the cone-gate diagonal to their post. As soon as this pass it made the receiver moves quickly to meet the pass, control it with 1-touch back in the direction of the goal, and take her shot immediately afterward. Without breaking stride (Important!), she continues to move in the direction of the Goal Keeper in anticipation of a mis-handled ball. As she approaches, the coach then rolls out a simulated botched save (rebound) for her to hunt and take a follow-up shot. Encourage her to *"Keep it on the ground!"*

After each player makes her pass or takes her shot, have them rotate in a clockwise manner to the next line. This rotation is meant to force training of both feet. So, make sure your players are receiving across the body with good first-touch and shooting with the same foot. This is meant to be a fast-paced exercise, so as soon as the follow-up shot is completed, have the next passer make her pass. Keeping the play moving quickly can mean each of your players getting a couple more shots on goal than they would otherwise not have had if everyone were walking.

Coaching Points:

- Keep passes on the ground so that they are controllable.
- Reinforce that the Goal Keeper *"is not your friend"*, so don't kick the ball straight to her. Encourage your players to shoot for the corners.

- Encourage 1 touch and then the shot. Don't give the Keeper time to close down the angle.

Manage the stations by the posts such that the player currently passing is not crowded and can provide a good pass. To help manage the queues at teach station, watch for players rotating in the wrong direction. If you have to, remind them which direction they are supposed to move and arbitrarily move some to empty stations. Tell them they should help balance the lines using their own initiative.

Quick review of the Danger Zone

Don't underestimate the power of a quick review of Danger Zone behavior just before your first game. Before you make field assignments and check in with the referees, walk your players out to the Danger Zone and spend just a few minutes quizzing them on what they should do when the ball is in this area. Make it important by making it a priority.

Fast-restart ball positioning

Prior to the game, you will want to get the Referees to approve 2-3 extra balls that you plan to utilize for fast restarts. Specifically, fast restarts on goal kicks where the ball is kicked so far out of the end-line that the other team has organized defensively by the time your Keeper has retrieved it. To avoid this, have one of your players spot a ball on either side of the goal your team is defending. Your Keeper can then grab and play one of these balls without delay. As soon as the ball goes out, your team should be yelling, *"Stretch!"* just like you have been practicing. Have a player currently sitting out go fetch the ball that went out and spot it back next to the post. There are no rules saying that the 'Home' team must provide the game ball; Visitors can provide balls as well. I have yet to encounter a referee that has denied this request for spotting pre-approved balls next to the posts.

Coaching during the game

On the side lines, what type of coach will you be? Will you be the one that sits in silence during the game? Or, will you be the coach that recognizes game-time for its unique training opportunities and guides your players where learning opportunities exist? The silent coach is typically a member of the 'Let them play' camp that subscribes to the philosophy of letting players figure it out for themselves. I can respect this approach, but I've seen a few too many silent coaches that seem to use the philosophy as a crutch for laziness, and even worse, apathetic behavior. Yes, apathy exists, but no one will ever admit to it. I have seen paid 'professional' coaches (with zero enthusiasm), deliver minimal corrections during my U11 daughter's practices and sit on their Duffs the entire game without saying a word.

It's my personal observation that teams with positive 'Guiding' coaches, sometimes referred to as a 'Joy Stick' coaches, generally experience greater success and more fun on the field. This has been my style of coaching and I have found that I need to do it less as each season progresses. This is because my players start to 'get it' and appropriately adjust their play with each game.

The operant word here, to distinguish yourself from the obnoxious coach that everyone talks about after the game, is 'positive.' Be sparring in your guidance and encouraging in your tone.   If you are screaming every time the ball changes direction, then your voice will essentially become noise in the background. Save your voice for things that matter, and there are plenty opportunities for this. For example, encourage your outside backs to push forward to take throw-ins. If opponents have a restart in your vicinity, encourage your players to encourage each other to mark appropriately. If your Goal Keeper is standing on her line when the ball is in the attacking third, ask her where she might position herself to help defend a counter-attack.   Many of these opportunities to make positive corrections and guidance simply don't exist outside of the full-sided game...so make what you have to say count.

Keep your guidance and corrections positive...even when it gets ugly. Resist *any* urge to make comments regarding a player's performance that is not constructive. For example, when the ball gets by your Goal Keeper, tell her to *"shake it off"* and that it takes *"a whole team to score a goal or prevent a goal."* If your striker's shot goes a little wide of the post, praise her aggressiveness in getting the shot off. If your defender loses a 1v1 with an attacker, be sure you praise her for coming out to meet the attack in the first place. The point being that reinforcing the good things that are happening, in spite of a bad outcome, will keep your players motivated to improve. Remember your promise to them at the beginning of the season to celebrate the risks they take.

Realistically, you can only be vocal for about half of the game. The reason? For the other half, your team is on other side of the field and most of them simply can't hear you. Save your breath, it's hardly worth trying. This is when you have to just settle-in, become the 'let them play' coach, and enjoy the game.

As a side note regarding the subject of winning and 'Joy Sticking' (Guiding) as a win-at-all-costs coaching philosophy...it doesn't have to be. I've never found anyone that's been able to tell me definitively when winning becomes important. Do an Internet search on this topic and you will find scores of experts citing surveys where youth players indicate 'winning' to be a lower priority than simply having fun. It's hard to argue this as a universal truth for us all, that we choose to do things that give us joy. Another truth that I have observed, repeatedly, is that winning is more joyous than losing. It's the team that leaves the field with the most points that is cheering and does what I call the 'Loser Tunnel' for the vanquished. It's the team that wins that runs down the side-line to high-five the parents. Be the positive, sparingly vocal, guiding coach that gives *your* team every advantage to experience this joy and become the gracious Victor.

Post-game recognition

In addition to your short post-game meeting, don't miss any opportunities to praise your players in post-game emails and texts to their parents. The parents will be proud, appreciative, and are sure to share the positive comments with their daughters. This praise is reinforcing for behavior and skills the you are teaching your players. What I have also found is that this type of communication 'banks goodwill' with the parents. Not being a perfect coach, there are sometimes decisions I make or things I do that can use a little forgiveness. Not missing any opportunities to praise and reinforce every player in some way buys me a little grace for the times that I screw up.

Here is an example of the types of emails that I regularly send out. This one was for the two players that shared Goal Keeping responsibilities throughout the season:

Email Subject Line: Be a leader in goal.

Hi Parents, please share this with your daughters as soon as possible.

SR and LB,

You both did a wonderful job playing Keeper this weekend. Were it not for the bravery and commitment on your part, the game could easily have gone in favor of our opponent.

As we move forward, your team is going to need you even more in the way of leadership in the backfield; especially as we continue to develop our skills as a team in 'playing-out-of-the-back' upon collecting the ball and goal kicks.

What I am asking of you going forward is that you take a lead in communicating to your Outside Backs (ahead of time) where they are supposed to be when you collect the ball or we have a goal kick and the team yells, "Stretch!". This is critically important because, if the Outside Backs are not in their proper positions, our chances of successfully getting the ball out of our defensive half is very low.

We had some very close calls because of this tendency of the Outside Backs to fall into old habits and 'drift forward' when we are taking a goal kick or distributing out after collection. When they do this, it becomes very easy for one player on the other team to mark two or more of our teammates. We experienced this while trying to play out of the back this weekend when the other team's forwards intercepted balls intended for our teammates and dribbled right back at us in goal. When our Outside Backs are in position (now your responsibility), this won't happen because you will have better options for distributing the ball.

Understand that communicating this to your Outside Backs is not 'being bossy', but rather being a leader and protecting your team from being taken advantage of on the field. Just use the right language to remind them of where they need to be when the team 'Stretches' into their attacking shape. For instance, you can simply say, "MD, I need you to be back even with me between the penalty box and touchline." Or, you could say, "EH, make sure you don't move forward on the punt or goal kick because I need you as an option here in the back." There will be players other than EH or MD playing Outside Back, so the important thing to remember is that THEY NEED YOU to communicate where they need to be for the team to be successful.

Be loud, be confident, and praise your defense when they perform. Developing this skill in orchestrating your defense is an important part of your future success as a Goal Keeper. I, Coach D, and the rest of your team appreciate your bravery and skill in the goal.

Coach Scott

Practice 4-1 – Email and Pre-Work:

This following practice was designed to help players get accustomed to controlling the ball on a fast surface. There is a likelihood that one (or more) of your games will be played on a turf field, which plays very differently than grass, or even more pronounced...on long grass. I have discovered that the next best thing to a turf field is an asphalt parking lot. If you don't have access to a parking lot, you can do most of these exercises on grass, with the exception of the 'Rolling Step-overs'. The rolling step-over exercise really does require a 'fast surface' to be conducted the way we desire. If you don't have access to any parking lot space (or tennis court) that you can lay claim to for 30 minutes, simply split those 10 minutes between the drills before and after.

Here is the email that I send out to parents the day before so that they are properly prepared. Though I typically supply soccer balls for regular training sessions, you will want players to bring their own so that it is not yours that are being scuffed-up on the asphalt.

Hi Parents,

*Please have the girls wear tennis shoes tonight **but also bring their cleats** to change into. We will be working on the black-top, training mostly tightly controlled dribbling and one-touch passing on the fast surface.*

Girls that are playing Goal Keeper, come to practice as early as you can so that we can practice some punting.

*Also, be sure to **BRING YOUR OWN BALL** tonight.*

Thanks,
Coach Scott

Practice 4-1: Foot skills on fast surface, directional first-touch, and training composure

This asphalt-based practice was originally developed to substitute for a soggy unplayable practice field. I now use it regularly to get players accustomed to faster ball speeds for playing on turf. You don't have to train on asphalt unless you want to, but I would highly recommend it if you have access to an unused parking lot. Even better, find some turf to train on if you can. Send out multiple messages to your team to make sure to wear tennis shoes but bring cleats. You will inevitably have one or two players show up with just their cleats.

(-30) GK Distributions - (In the grass) Start with bowling-style distributions. Get them used to tucking the ball against the inside of their forearm for control and distributing far enough out that friction from the grass doesn't eat all of the energy of the ball. 15 minutes in, start working on punt technique into the nets. Ensure that GKs are taking 2-3 steps and releasing the ball no higher than mid-thigh.

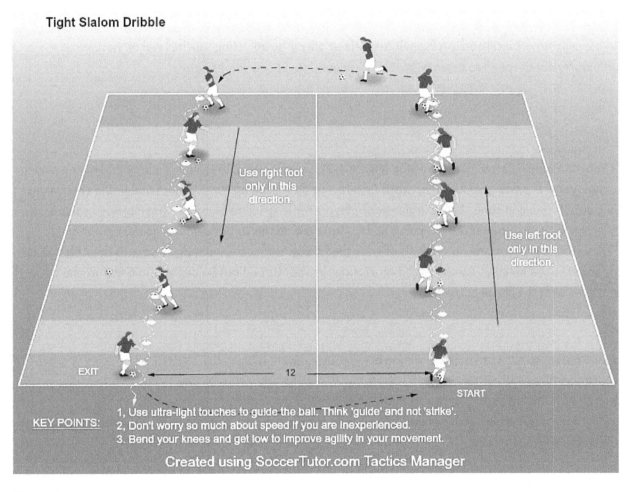

Figure 4-1

(10) Tight Slalom Dribble – (On asphalt if available) Setup a two parallel lines (12 adult paces of separation) of exactly 13 cones spaced 2 short adult paces apart as shown in Figure 4-1. Have players form a line at the end of one line so that after a player dribbles through one line of cones, they simply dribble over to the opposite side and start dribbling back in the opposite direction. Don't wait for the current dribbler to get more than 3-4 cones through the slalom before sending the next dribbler; one of your major goals is to keep players moving and productive. You can even put down a different colored cone and indicate it as the point at which the next dribbler starts. Be sure to demonstrate for your players what technique you want to see. Call out the small touches and agile movement through cones using light, fast touches.

Progressions:

1. Dribble one direction with left foot only; Dribble the opposite direction with the right foot.
2. After about 5 minutes, allow player to use both feet as comfortable.
3. Make it a competition! Make it exciting! Get your stopwatch out to see who can get through both lines the fastest without missing a cone. Maybe even announce that the winner will race the assistant coach in a championship!

Coaching Points:

- The ball will move quickly on the asphalt (or turf) so only little adjusting touches will be necessary.
- Don't worry about speed to begin with. Focus on control. Speed comes later.

(8) Partner Short Passing – Partner short-passing (Figure 4-2) is simple 1 & 2-touch quick passing between players to improve their general passing skills. Adjust your field layout by picking up every other cone in the two slalom lines starting with the second cone. This will give your players some space to organize. Have players square-off with a partner, facing each other about 4-5 paces apart. They can do this in-between the cones setup for dribbling. They should be bouncing on the balls of their feet ready to receive and make a pass to their teammate. Don't worry about speed initially. Focus instead on getting the foot turned out 90 degrees in order to make a good straight pass with the inside of the foot.

Progressions:

1. 2 touch passes to each other. Take a controlling touch and then pass back.
2. 1 touch passes to each other.
3. Turn the foot inward and make passes with the outside of the foot.
4. Finally, make it a competition! Get your stopwatch out and see which pair can complete the most passes to each other in one minute.

Coaching Points:

Receive and pass using the most convenient foot (i.e., the side the ball was passed to). DO NOT adjust to use the dominant foot. You must enforce this practice if you expect your players to reach higher levels of control and passing on the field. Let them know it's normal to feel awkward as they learn, but that awkwardness will go away with practice.

Partner Short Passing

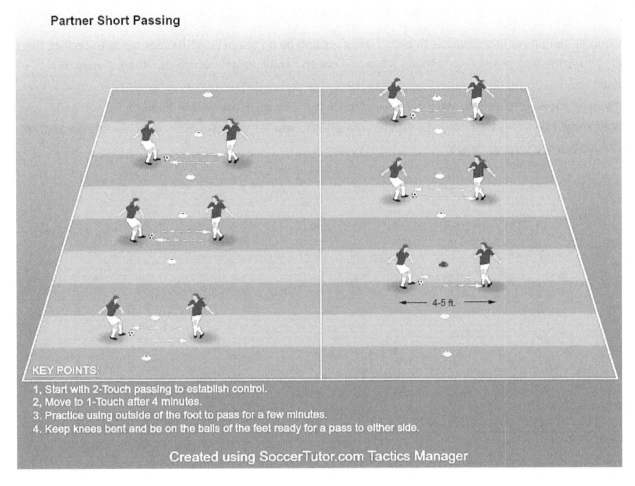

KEY POINTS:
1. Start with 2-Touch passing to establish control.
2. Move to 1-Touch after 4 minutes.
3. Practice using outside of the foot to pass for a few minutes.
4. Keep knees bent and be on the balls of the feet ready for a pass to either side.

Created using SoccerTutor.com Tactics Manager

Figure 4-2

(12) 3 Player Agility Passing - This is a good drill for raising the energy level and reaction time of your players. It's basically a two-ball passing exercise with three players. The two players on the ends of the passing channel take turns making passes to a player in the middle. The player in the middle makes a 1-touch pass back to the player on the outside and quickly turns 180 degrees to receive a pass from the opposite player. Players on the outside need to take a controlling touch on the ball and time their pass to the middle player as she completes her own pass and starts to turn.

To run this drill, utilize the cones that you have already have in place. Your passing lanes should be about 4 paces wide. There should be 7 cones remaining in each line of cones, creating enough 3-player passing lanes for a team of 12. Time is precious, so have your assistant coach lay out two balls for each passing lane and you should quickly assign players to each station. Position the balls on top of each outside cone so that they are ready to go. Be sure to rotate players on the outsides after 3 minutes.

Progressions:

After everyone gets a turn in the middle, make it a competition to see which team can make the most passes in one minute. Have them quickly decide who is in the middle for their team and then start.

Coaching Points:

- Encourage the player in the middle to bend her knees and be on the balls of the feet ready to receive the ball. This is the best position to respond when she doesn't know exactly which side the ball may be passed to.
- Encourage speed-of-play with quick passes and quick turns by the player in the middle.
- Passes should be firmly weighted. Explain to your players why weak/slow passes only give the competitor more time to catch up to the ball.

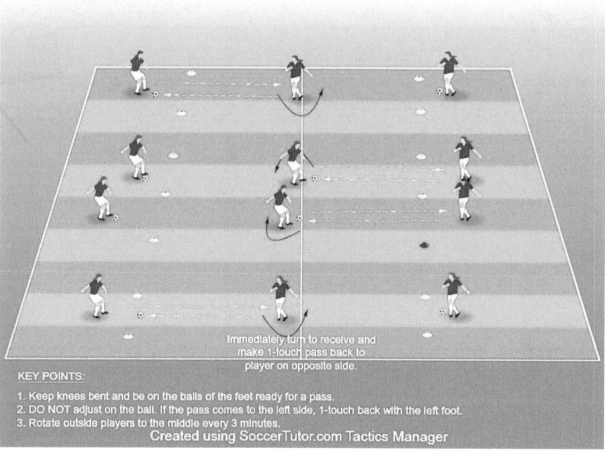

3 Player Agility Passing

Immediately turn to receive and make 1-touch pass back to player on opposite side.

KEY POINTS:

1. Keep knees bent and be on the balls of the feet ready for a pass.
2. DO NOT adjust on the ball. If the pass comes to the left side, 1-touch back with the left foot.
3. Rotate outside players to the middle every 3 minutes.

Created using SoccerTutor.com Tactics Manager

Figure 4-3

(10) Rolling Step-Overs – (On asphalt if available) This is a great exercise for training timing of a step-overs on a ball in motion. In the spaces between (or on the outside of) the parallel lines, your players will execute running step-overs in the long direction. Have two lanes working next to each other, but not too close that they interfere with each other. The players should be queued beside the coaches. The first player stands in front of coach with legs about shoulder width apart. The coach then serves the first ball forward through the legs at a pace appropriate for safely executing the move on the pavement. Players execute as many moving step-overs as they can before the ball loses speed and they have to take another light touch. Speed is not the objective at this point, but rather timing execution and good form. Demonstrate what this skill looks like with the help of your assistant coach.

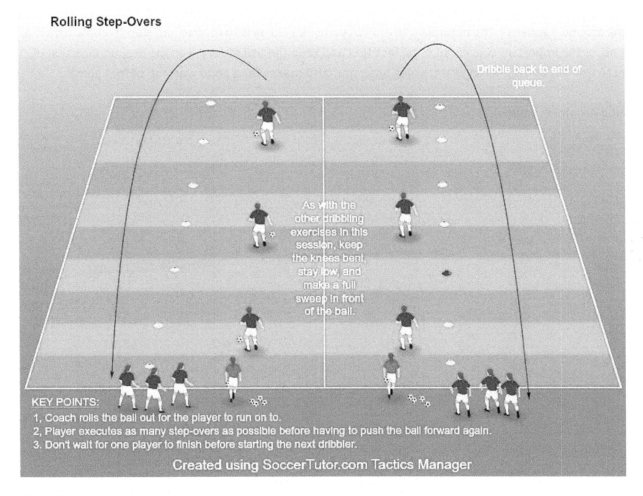

Figure 4-4

An **important note** regarding layout for this drill: If you are training on an asphalt surface, ensure that the directional layout is such that any slope present supports the ball rolling straight in the direction of the dribble. If the ball immediately starts pulling to the left or right, you are degrading the effectiveness of the drill.

Progressions:

As players develop a bit of comfort with the step-over action, encourage them to be quicker and see how many step-overs they can perform before the ball reaches the end of the dribbling channel.

Coaching Points:

- Correct each player to use good form in the step-over. The leg should sweep around the front of the ball on the outside-to-inside movement.

- Encourage your players to bend their knees and get lower to make their move. Have them get their hands out to help with their balance.

(15) Passing around a square – The natural inclination of younger players is to receive and stop the ball. This is a drill that teaches the important concept of using first-touch to keep the ball moving into the desired direction of play. You can use this drill during regular training time, or it **also makes for a good warmup before games**.

Passing Around A Square

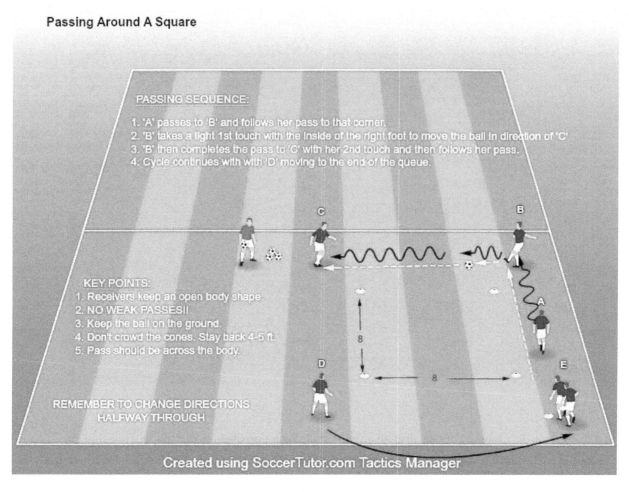

Figure 4-5

Lay out as many squares (Figure 4-5) of 8 adult paces as will support groups of 5 players. If you have fewer than 15 players, distribute them evenly between two stations. Start with a queue and ball on one corner and one player on each of the remaining corners. The player in the front of the queue will pass across the body of the next player in a counter-clockwise fashion and follow her pass to the next corner. That player receives the ball across the body, and with the inside of her right foot, applies 1st touch that sets her up for the next pass. When moving in the counter-clockwise direction, players should only be using their right foot to receive and make a pass. With the right foot typically being the dominant foot of players, they should be able to make these passes reasonably well and with confidence. Be sure to switch to the clockwise direction to train the left foot receiving.

Coaching Points:

- Players tend to 'crowd the cones' during this drill. Have them focus on staying back from the cone at least 4-5 feet to enable plenty of room to receive with an open body shape.
- Encourage adjusting to the ball to receive across the body even if the pass is not perfect.
- Encourage a properly weighted (speed) pass that doesn't run out of speed and just makes it to the player on the other corner. The ball must arrive with enough pace (speed) that the receiving player can touch it, without much effort, into the desired direction and keep play moving quickly. Consider this 1st touch as a 'controlled ricochet' with the inside of the foot into the desired direction.

To add a little positive pressure, make it a competition between the stations toward the end. See which group can complete the most passes around the square in 60 seconds. 3-4 laps in 60 seconds seems to be a normal count for this age group. Make sure both groups are passing in the same direction to keep the competition fair. The ball must travel on the outside of all cones for the lap to count.

Break, change into cleats, and move onto grass...

(25) Touch to Space - This training takes-on what I consider one of the most pervasive problems in youth soccer, which is the tendency for young players to haphazardly kick the ball away. 'Kick Ball' as it is not so affectionately referred to. This behavior doesn't just happen in recreational play, but also in competitive (club) environments. This drill recreates a commonly occurring situation on the field where players typically panic and kick the ball away. With deliberate practice, you can help your players develop the composure necessary for winning 50/50 challenges and keeping possession for their team.

This commonly occurring situation is a race to the ball where competitors arrive at the ball nearly simultaneously. When this happens, the inexperienced player that barely gets there first, but has no time to properly receive or take control of the ball, will most often launch the ball into 'Nowhere Land'...creating yet another 50/50 opportunity somewhere else on the field. So many times, soccer can be measured in split-seconds for decision making, and this is one of those times. Your task is to train your players to exercise control in this split-second of time and take a measured touch on the ball into safe space on either side of the competitor. If they can win the race and take this light controlling touch, their momentum through the challenge into the opposite direction should enable them to take control of the ball and retain possession.

As timing is absolutely critical in this drill, you (Coach) will setup and control the 50/50 challenge to ensure that your players win and are able to successfully execute the desired behavior. For now, DO NOT delegate the responsibility of the pressuring opponent to one of your players. You must do this yourself to ensure that your attacker barely beats you to the ball. For every cycle they don't get to the ball first, they have missed an opportunity to become more effective. Their teammates are not mentally inclined to allow anyone to get to the ball first, and you really don't want to train this mindset anyway. During the drill, encourage your players to 'go hard' and 'be first to the ball.' Don't lose the race for the free ball!

Touch to Space

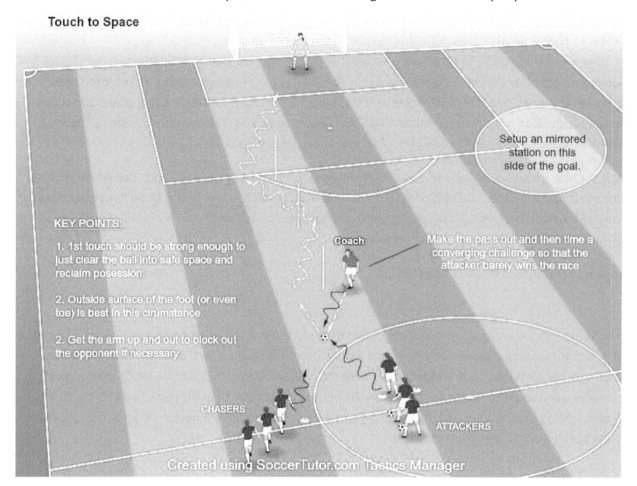

Setup an mirrored station on this side of the goal.

KEY POINTS:

1. 1st touch should be strong enough to just clear the ball into safe space and reclaim posession.

2. Outside surface of the foot (or even toe) is best in this cirumstance.

2. Get the arm up and out to block out the opponent if necessary.

Coach

Make the pass out and then time a converging challenge so that the attacker barely wins the race

CHASERS

ATTACKERS

Created using SoccerTutor.com Tactics Manager

Figure 4-6

A VERY IMPORTANT EXCEPTION: This new expectation of taking the controlling touch needs to be delivered with a bit of context. If your players win a split-second race to the ball within the danger area in their defending-third, the expectation is STILL a one-touch clearance out to the side or up the field for safety. If the ball is outside of the DANGER ZONE, always seek to control it as you are training today.

Following the diagram in Figure 4-6, setup two slalom lines similar to the ones practiced in Week 1. In addition to the element of pressure provided by Defender (Chaser), this drill also adds a finishing (goal scoring) opportunity for the dribbler and goal keeping opportunities for your GKs. Training GKs is one of the weakest links in most training programs due to the limited time available and the specialized nature of the training. This is unfortunate given the impact a good Keeper can have on the success of the team. Never miss an opportunity to incorporate Keeper training into your schedule!

Evenly divide your players between the Attacker and Chaser queues as illustrated. Make sure that all players have a pinnie hanging out of the back of their shorts for the chasers to pull. It doesn't make any difference what color it is so don't waste time dickering over what color to use. Don't worry if you have an extra player on one queue or the other; numbers rarely work out perfectly anyway.

As the Coach, position yourself just inside and slightly behind the first coaching stick. This is an important detail as you will be making the pass out at a slight angle and forcing your player to take her controlling touch toward the outside. Follow your pass out with fast, yet passive-pressure, that places you on top of the ball at about the same time. Your pass out should be with just enough pace that you meet in the middle. This then sets her up to take the light touch forward, regain control, and practice her changes-of-direction through the sticks on her way to the goal. With this configuration, your players should take their controlling touch with the most convenient foot when they win the race.

Provide a demonstration of how the drill is supposed to look. You and your assistant coach should have conferred with each other beforehand to present a good example; It doesn't matter who plays which role. You can have one of the players chase you through the sticks as a defender, trying to steal your pinnie before you get to goal. The Attacker should start sprinting to meet the ball as soon as it is in motion. The most critical detail of this effort is timing your interception of the Attacker so that she barely wins. This is what we want on the field. Your attacker may even have to make somewhat of a leap into the air to avoid an opponent's foot or leg, so encourage them to be prepared for some gymnastics.

Each Attacker in the queue at the cone gate should have her own ball. Chasers need no ball. Have the next Attacker pass you her ball in preparation for her turn. This quick preparation should be done while the other side is making their run. As coach, your job is to keep the energy level up, so make sure that you have a ball ready for the next run and ensure no time is wasted. If you are leisurely in your pace of execution, you can easily miss 2-3 additional opportunities for each player to work on this important skill.

Make sure to have Attackers/Chasers switch roles after each run. In the last 10 minutes, have the groups switch sides and do the same thing. By switching sides, you are giving them the opportunity to experience the opposite angle of approach and perhaps use their non-dominant foot to take their controlling touch and eventual shot on goal.

Chasers can start their pursuit immediately after the Attacker takes her controlling touch into space. The Chaser must follow the Attacker through the sticks in the wake of her dribble. They cannot take short-cuts in their effort to steal the pinnie.

If you have more than one Goal Keeper that you are training, make sure that they are taking turns in the goal fielding shots from the Attackers. If you have a third coach, or just another parent helping for this session, have them back with the Keepers to encourage them to come off of their line and close down the angle of attack as the Attackers come around the last stick.

Coaching Points:

- The key to winning the 50/50 challenge is to have an all-out mentality in the race for the ball and to not let up. Keep running through the play and keep going.
- Most young players have been conditioned to using the inside of their foot to make passes. Make sure that players know that they can use any surface of their foot to move the ball into safe space during their controlling touch. In this circumstance, a light touch of the toe or the outside of the foot is often the best choice.

Practice 4-2: More throw-in strategy, 1v1+GK, give-n-go, 6v6 SSG unstructured

Optional light workout (1 hour) before tomorrow's game scheduled on our regular practice day. (6 girls attended)

(20) Throw-in w/ fleet-screening opponent – This throw-in instruction was wasn't originally on my training schedule and was motivated watching some Select U14 tournament-play over the weekend. My younger daughter's club team is very good, but they were dominated by a single competitor on multiple levels in the final of this tournament. Of particular note, was this competitor's ability to retain possession on throw-ins. I was intrigued enough to craft an email to the coach of that team, asking outright about how they train throw-ins. Here is that email:

Greetings Ms. Successful Coach,

We've never met, but I coach recreational soccer in Loveland and am hoping you might indulge a quick question about throw-ins.

I had the opportunity to watch your team at the Party-on-the-Pitch tournament. I was so impressed by the ability of your team to retain possession during throw-ins that I studied them more closely. I watched the first throw-in and it appeared that the receiver screened/shielded the defender while the ball was thrown (with impeccable timing) across the body in the direction of the goal. I watched the second throw-in... same technique. Then, when I saw the third and subsequent throw-ins, with the same result, I suspected that it was a trained skill. This was done with such fluidity, that not a single foul was called for impeding play. For the game that I watched, I estimate that your team retained possession over 70% of the time...which is pretty darned good.

Is this technique is actively trained throughout your club, or is this just training that you have delivered personally for your own team? If you could point me to some type of training reference for this technique, I'd be most appreciative; I'd like to teach it to my own team.

Sincerely,
Scott Wheeler

It's not surprising that I never heard back from this coach either way. In the arena of competitive soccer, I can imagine that most coaches/clubs would want their internal training practices/methods to remain confidential, particularly if those methods 'pushed the envelope' with respect to rules. I didn't really need confirmation that this was part of their training; What I observed worked and would definitely be incorporated into my own training.

This training isn't complicated. At the youth level, what you typically have happening is one defensive player closely marking an attacking player. As the attacker moves, the defender will jockey to position herself in front of the attacker and cut her off from receiving the throw. Well-trained defenders will position themselves 'goal-side' of the attacker when marking, but this generally isn't always the case at the U11 level. At any rate, this dance continues for whatever amount of time it takes for an attacker to get free or for the thrower to feel pressured enough to release the ball.

What you want to train with this technique is a mutual understanding between thrower and receiver as to what will 'trigger' the throw and where it will be made. During this intense jockeying, the thrower needs to have the ball at-the-ready behind her head. She needs to be watching for the exact moment that her teammate effectively fleet-screens the defender so that she can make her throw. When the receiver is executing this screening action, her arms need to be out wide and down...signaling that she is 'ready' for the throw. This is the 'trigger' for the throw-in that the thrower must not miss. In this instance, the ball should be thrown across the body of the receiver for her to run on. The throw needs to be properly weighted so that the receiver can be first to the ball and retain possession.

You can setup multiple stations to practice this throw. To help train your Goal Keepers, you can even turn it into a shooting drill where the receiver takes the ball to the goal. Either way, the thrower becomes the defender and the defender becomes the receiver in the sequence. Instruct the defenders to defend at 50-75% effort to help train the timing between thrower and receiver. Let them know that they are helping to train their teammates by allowing the throw.

As indicated above, this practice was only attended by 6 players that learned the skill. During our game the following day, I had one player that was effectively screening a competitor during a throw-in, except the thrower was taking forever to release the ball. The player performing the throw-in had no idea what was happening as she was not at the practice when this tactic was taught. Her teammate was consequently called for a foul for impeding play and we turned the ball over. The lesson here is to make sure that everyone is present when you are teaching such tactics as everyone must understand their role in successful execution.

(20) Touch to Space 1v1 +GK – This is a multi-purpose drill that supports the ongoing behavioral objectives of taking an agile touch into safe space when competing for 50/50 balls. To help players develop composure under pressure, you've got to subject them to controlled pressure where they are setup to win.

This exercise is similar to the 'Touch to Space' practice in Session 4-1, but turns it into a 1v1+GK (1 Attacker vs. 1 Defender + GK). The coach is at the endline and about 5 yards away from the post with a queue of defenders waiting to compete for the ball. Another queue of attackers is waiting at the top of the 18-yard box to win a race for the ball. Play begins when the coach passes the ball into the space between the next attacker and defender in the queues.

The weight (speed) of the pass is critical to setting-up the attacker for success. Your job as the coach is to know the capabilities (speed) of your players and to make a pass that the attacker will reach just a couple of steps before the defender. You can either roll the ball out or pass it with the foot, whichever you are more comfortable with. This will be challenging and it might take you some practice to get it right, so push the ball a little further out for starters as you dial-in your passes.

Touch to Space - 1v1 With Goal Keeper

Attackers

KEY POINTS:
1. Go 'all out' for the ball.
2. Don't let challenges run more than 20 seconds.
3. Play ends with a shot on goal or a defensive clearance.
4. KEEP THE BALL ON THE GROUND!

Create a second station of opposite configuration on the other side of the field if you are able. Rotate players between stations after 10 min.

Coach

Defenders

Created using SoccerTutor.com Tactics Manager

Figure 4-7

Once the ball is in play, the defender's job is to clear the ball from the danger area and the attacker's job is to score a goal. Emphasize to the attacker that her job is to get to the ball first and maintain control by taking a light touch into space, thus keeping possession and creating an opportunity to score. The attacker can take her shot whenever she has the chance, even if it's a result of you pushing the ball out too far initially. Rotate your Goal Keepers out with each cycle so that they all field an even amount of shots.

Encourage your Attackers to keep the ball on the ground and look for the corners. I can't count the number of shots in youth soccer that I have seen sail wide and high of the goal from this training distance. Shots on the ground are generally harder to save unless struck directly to the Keeper.

If you are fortunate enough to have a whole field, set a station up on the 2nd goal so that you can get more cycles of training in.

(20) 2vCoach+GK - Use this drill train offsides awareness and a variant of the classic 'Give-n-Go' interaction to penetrate defense. Set two lines of attackers approximately 20 yards out from the goal as laid out in Figure 4-8. One line will have a ball and initiate the attack. The attackers will come out in pairs against a Coach offering semi-passive defending. You could send a player out to defend, but you want to take advantage of the role yourself in order to coach your attacker as to when to make her move. As coach, you will also be able to 'practice what you preach' and provide a good example of defensive close-down. Defend in such a way as to force a pass to the supporting attacker. Encourage quick shots on goal after the first pass. Make sure the attackers understand the concept of off-sides and cannot be behind the last defender at the time the pass is made. Passes should be made into space for the second attacker to run onto. Attackers should switch sides to practice dribbling and making the through pass. After 10 minutes, switch the ball to start from the opposite side work the opposite foot.

Figure 4-8

Coaching Points:

- Attackers – Don't pass too early. Dribble in and pull the defender away from your teammate before you make your pass.
- Attackers - Ensure that the attacker passing to supporting teammate sprints past the defender to continue supporting the attack. Your job as an attacker is never finished; sprint forward to receive a potential cross back from your teammate.
- Attackers – Ensure you are using good dribbling technique and keeping the ball close to the foot.

- Goal Keepers – Make sure you are paying attention and watching the direction of the play and which way it might shift if the ball is passed. Come off your line and meet the attacker to close-down the angle of attack.

(30) 6v6 SSG w/ Kick-Off Restart - As indicated at the top of this section, this happened to be a short practice with a limited number of players on this day. if you have the extra 30 minutes available, run the basic 6v6 SSG (Reference Practice 3-1) with the following progression:

1. As best you can, set your players up with two sides that reflect positions they will be playing in the game.
2. Use formal kick-off to restart after each goal and make sure they start with a back-pass to ensure possession.
3. Before the restart, point out to your defending wide mid-fielders that their job is to mark their counterparts to ensure they don't receive a pass on the kick-off. Or better, to mark inconspicuously enough that they can intercept any pass.

Coaching Points: Encourage lots of support but focus on the outside mid marking on restarts.

Practice 5-1: Pre-practice headers, foot skills/fakes, teach them how to run, 6v6 SSG (Marking)

Layout the multi-purpose field indicated in Figure 1-1. Today, your players will begin learning how to run. You will develop a baseline of their performance from which to evaluate their improvement. Hence, the length-wise side of 6 cones on the multi-purpose layout needs to be exactly 20 yards today for the sake of consistently measuring performance. This same layout will be used for the foot-skills training, so lay down additional cone-sets as necessary to accommodate more than 12 players. Make sure to pick these cone-sets back up before you begin the sprint training. Lay down two cones a bit further out from the end of the 20-yard mark to serve as targets for your runners; otherwise, they will start to let-up as they approach the cone marking 20 yards.

(-30) Punt Practice - Have your Goal Keepers (GK) show up early if possible and work with them on low-trajectory punts. Work on getting them comfortable running up to the edge of the 18-yard line to release their punt. Emphasize that you want them punting in the direction of the opponent's corner flag and not down the middle. The reason for this is that the middle part of the field generally contains the strongest players and is the most congested. Punting down the middle, unless your GK has a magnificent punt, reduces your odds of retaining possession. Have one Coach at the 18-yard line giving corrections.

(-15) Header Training - Fewer aspects of the game are as sensitive as the topic of heading. While everyone agrees that minimizing the risk of concussion is important, the hypersensitivity surrounding this skill seems to have most youth coaches hesitant to teach it at all. As of February 16, 2019, the US Youth Soccer (USYS) policy regarding headers is that no player 10 or younger may head the ball at all (USYS, 2019). Those between the ages of 11 and 12 may head the soccer ball in a game, but are limited to no more than 25 headers per week in the training environment. This is policy set by the national governing body, you will want to check with your local club director to determine if your club's policy is more restrictive.

As indicated, my personal observation has been that coaches are hesitant to teach anything extensive in the way of heading at the U11-U13 levels. A subsequent observation is the unrealistic expectation that players be able to head the ball into the net from a corner set-piece upon their 12th birthday. Most coaches would deny having this expectation, but I've seen it first-hand on multiple occasions. I've seen recreational coaches have players, with little or no experience heading, clustered at the mid-field line while they punt from the 18-yard line and encourage them to head the ball. In a similar fashion, I've seen experienced club coaches serve hard corners to players after only limited short-distance training, and not surprisingly, only 1/20 services find a player's head. This is because they are 'scared to death' of the ball, and rightfully so.

Heading is not a skill that can just be 'switched on' when players reach an approved age. It's a skill that takes courage, and that courage needs to be developed progressively over a reasonable period of time. You can begin training this skill responsibly, at this level, and better prepare your players for the day that all restrictions are lifted. Delivering this training represents another commitment to 'player development', as you are not likely to see these skills used during your current season.

If you haven't already introduced heading to your players, this is the approach that I use:

Start with a soft ball that your players can be comfortable with. The ball that I start with is a Tachikara® SS32 Soft Kick Soccer Ball. These are great if you can still find them. They have a cloth outer layer, a rubber bladder, and are very soft on the head. I have also used the *Heading Trainer* ball offered by TheTrainingTriangle.com. Both of these balls are about half the weight of a normal soccer ball, which greatly reduces impact forces.

Get familiar with proper heading technique and plan a schedule of progression. There are a ton of video-based references available on the Internet you can use to educate yourself. One of the best that I have found is a YouTube® production by Pro Tips 4U™ that features USWNT legend Abby Wambach explaining the progression that she learned on. The following Internet search should net you this instructional on the first page.

Internet Search Terms/Phrase for Skill Videos: SOCCER TIPS: HOW TO PROPERLY HEAD THE BALL WITH ABBY WAMBACH

If you have been using this training curriculum from the previous season, you will already have progressed to the standing header. If not, start training at a level that makes sense for your players.

Split your players in to two groups as they arrive to practice. Arrange themselves in a semi-circle around each coach to receive an underhanded toss to head. If possible, have less experienced players with one coach and more experienced players with the other. It could be that you start serving at a small distance of 6' as you introduce the skill. You may find that some players completely flinch/duck the ball when you lob it in their direction; For these players, move in a little closer and give encouragement. You may even let them hold the ball and head it to you to get started. The important consideration is to be flexible and supportive in building their confidence. As they grow more confident, increase your distance.

Here is a general sequence of good form to follow when heading:

1. Set a firm stance with one leg slightly forward and knees bent.
2. Arms up and out to the side ready to pull back.
3. Back slightly arched.
4. Tighten from the neck to the core when striking the ball.
5. Keep the eyes open.
6. Attack and strike the ball with the forehead.
7. Pull the arms back and thrust the head forward with ferocity.

Coaching Points:

- Know the age of each player and ensure that no one under 11 heads the ball at all.
- Don't force participation as this is a pre-practice activity. You will likely find that you can't hold most players back as they find this activity fun and challenging.
- Not more than 30 min. per week.
- Do not use a regulation ball; Use a soft indoor ball or the specialized 'Heading Trainer'
- Encourage them stop at any time they feel uncomfortable.
- Challenge them to head the ball over the top of your own head!

(30) Foot-Skills - Setup a General Foot Skills Practice Area according to diagram 1-1. Ensure that the first and last dribbling-lines in one row are spaced exactly 20 yards apart. These will be used for timing the sprints.

(10) Dribbling Step-Overs - Revisit the static Step-Over to reinforce the basic movements. This drill will graduate your players to performing the step-over while dribbling and taking the ball away in the opposite direction with the inside of the foot. The basic movement is to dribble toward the cone using small touches with the outside of the foot (or toe-down Messi style) and perform the step-over with that same foot. There are a couple of reasons for using the same foot: #1) In a live situation, this will be the side furthest from a defender that is challenging for the ball, and #2) the distance of the step-over is shorter, making it easier to complete and change directions.

10 minutes might seem like a long time for this drill, but many will still be struggling to master the basic movement. The single biggest issue to watch for is not completing a sweep all the way around ball, thus preventing and effective pivot in the opposite direction. Be sure to use this extra time to walk around to give corrections and do demonstrations for individual players that still need help.

(10) Figure 8s - Dribble with the outside of the foot when moving between cones. Your players will thrive with a little bit of pressure. Announce that there will be a competition afterwards and that there will be a prize. It seems like every season I have and extra ball lying around that I can give away as a prize. I have also bought inexpensive pairs of 'crazy socks' that the players get excited about; it's money well spent.

1st Progression: First turns are performed using the inside of the foot, taking 2-3 smaller chops on the ball to work it around the cone. Reverse direction and perform the chops around the opposite cone with the inside of the other foot.

2nd Progression: Move to cutting around the cone with the outside of the foot. Change directions and perform the cuts with the outside of the opposite foot.

3rd Progression: Finish with a competition to see who can dribble around the most cones in 60 seconds. Players can use either the inside or outside of their foot when dribbling around the cone, but must use the instep or the outside of their foot when dribbling between cones. The 'honor system' applies here with each player counting for themselves.

(10) Inside Cuts on the move - This is also another graduation point where your players move from performing the inside-cut (chop fakes) in a stationary position to performing it with forward movement. This is one of the most fundamental and effective fakes in the game of soccer and, at the same time, I believe one of the most under-trained.

Inside Cuts On-the-Move

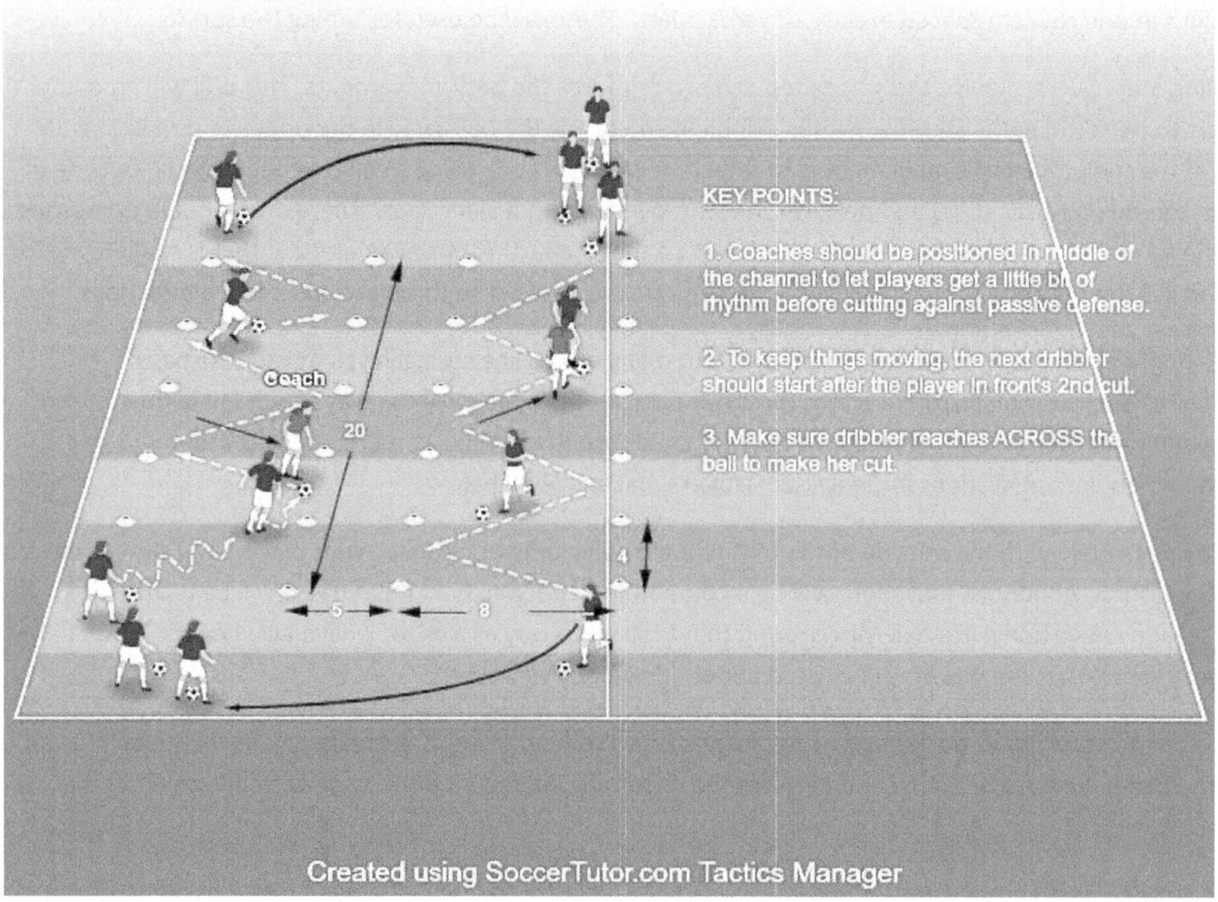

KEY POINTS:

1. Coaches should be positioned in middle of the channel to let players get a little bit of rhythm before cutting against passive defense.

2. To keep things moving, the next dribbler should start after the player in front's 2nd cut.

3. Make sure dribbler reaches ACROSS the ball to make her cut.

Created using SoccerTutor.com Tactics Manager

Figure 5-1

Queue your players up on one end of the 20-yard dribbling channel and have them start their dribble. The next player can start when the player in front of her reaches the middle of the channel. They should be dribbling side-to-side in a zig-zag fashion. When they are dribbling to the left, they should be using the outside (pinky toe) of their left foot. When they get close to the cones they should then reach **across and ahead of** the ball with their left foot and cut the ball back across the body at an angle and with just enough pace that they can control it and start the dribble with the outside of their right foot. Moving to the right mirrors the movements used on the left.

As the coach, you should position yourself in about the middle of the channel as a passive defender challenging for the ball. The extent of your defensive efforts should really be no more than to provide a 'warm body' that converges in the direction of ball travel. As with the 'Touch to Space' drill, your job here is to help your players develop a sense of timing in executing the chop back across the body. Have your assistant coach position him/herself in the middle of the other channel and serving the same role. As players exit one channel, they dribble over to and back through the other channel. Focus on timing and rhythm over speed at this point.

Be vocal and give plenty of corrections; your players won't get better if they don't know they are performing the skill incorrectly. The key things to watch for are:

Coaching Points:

- The chop back across the body needs to be tight. Players learning this skill have a tendency to cut-back at an angle that is too wide and allows for a defender to get a foot on the ball, thus destroying the fake. The angle shouldn't be very much, almost lateral in-fact.

- In order for this fake to work, the ball has to be slightly ahead of the dribbler and the next touch must look like an intended touch in the same direction, otherwise, the defender is going to back-off and you won't be able to use her momentum against her. What commonly happens during this drill is that your players will get their whole body on the opposite side of the ball before they take a touch in the opposite direction. And when they do, it's not even a chop, but rather a simple touch with the inside of the foot. This fools no one. Watch for and correct this behavior immediately; otherwise, you are wasting time and allowing development of bad technique.

- In addition to the tight angle, the ball needs to be cut back across the body with just enough pace (force) to beat the defender. In the excitement of the moment, 'dialing-back' the force with which the ball is struck takes discipline and composure. If the ball is struck with too much force, it generally arrives at the feet of a nearby defender.

(30) Sprint Instruction - There is a correlation between how fast your players are collectively and how much success they will enjoy on the field. In delivering sprint instruction to your players, you can help them run about 10% faster (on average) almost immediately. Imagine your whole team running 10% faster with not more than 60 minutes of instruction. Imagine how much faster they can be on the ball and how much more pressure they can bring to their opponents.

This is the beginning of sprint instruction/training for your team to pick up this awesome 'low hanging fruit.' If you observe closely, you will see that just about all of your players this age (especially girls) display poor form when running, with the arm-motion being the most obvious culprit. This is because no one has ever taught them how to run.

You don't have to be a certified speed trainer to help your players run faster, you just need to be able to communicate several simple improvements layered over the next 3-4 weeks. This training begins with proper arm movement and hand position.

One small addition to your foot-skills training layout to help with the sprints should be placement of a 'target cone' about 5 yards beyond the actual 20-yard mark. When you do run these sprints, instruct them to run hard toward this marker so that they don't 'let up' as they approach the 20-yard mark.

(5) Develop a baseline - Individually, have each girl run the 20-yard dash as fast as she can using her current running form. These sprints are conducted through the dribbling channel that you just finished using for inside cuts on-the-move. Tell them to just do the best they can. This gives us a baseline for assessing the level of improvement we hope to realize after instructing proper technique. Time and record the run for each player. Split them into two lines and have the assistant coach time girls in the second line. They are not racing each other, so start the time of each player separately. To standardize how times are recorded, ensure that you and your assistant coach start time immediately *after* you say the word "Go!" (not at the time you say "Go") and stop time when their body crosses the line. Consistency in your method is the key.

(10) Arm-pump Instruction: Keep it simple...elbows at 90 degrees, hands open/relaxed, and pump straight with hands extending 'cheek-to-cheek' (as in butt cheek to face cheek). Have the girls form a circle around you for demonstration purposes and instructing the basic movement. Rotate in the middle so that each girl can see your arms in the starting position and how straight the form needs to be. Expect to correct a lot of bad form where the elbows are turned out or otherwise different from what is described above.

Explain to them how any motion across the body 'steals' speed from them. So, it's super important to keep everything straight and moving forward.

While still in this circle, ensure their hips are square to the middle of the circle. Their back leg should be straight and for now their front leg should be bent such that their shin is perpendicular to the ground (i.e., straight up/down). Hands should be in the check-to-cheek starting position with the hand opposite the forward leg being next to the face. On your command of 'Go!', have the girls see how quickly they can single-pump their arms to the opposite position. Do this several times and then move to 2 pumps. Do 2 pumps several times and then move to 3 pumps.

Next, have them pump their arms continuously at a progressively faster pace using the example of shifting gears in a car (for those having ever driven a stick). Start slowly in 1st gear and maintain for 10-15 seconds, then shift to 2nd gear and hold it for 10-15 seconds, etc. Don't wear them out as use of these muscle groups is probably new for many of them.

Ask them if they would like to now put their new running technique to work to see if they can improve their 20-yard sprint times. You should get a resounding *"Yes!"*.

(15) Re-run times to evaluate immediate improvement. Everyone wants to be fast and you are going to be pleasantly surprised at how eager each player will be to become faster. They will want to know immediately after they run if they beat their last time. For a 12-player roster, you have enough time to run each player about 4 times.

Make sure you record these times in a spreadsheet that can be sorted from fastest to slowest, as you will be using these times for subsequent matchups. For instance, the next time you run sprints, positions 1 &2 will line up next to each other, then 3 & 4 match up, etc. This way nobody gets 'blown out' and the players are able to offer positive pressure to each other.

(20) SSG Marking Game - 6v6 on a short field. If you have full-field availability, and you are allowed to move goals, bring one goal to midfield and play with half the field. If you have players that like to play Keeper, let them play in each of the goals to get some action. Otherwise, coaches play the role of GK. If you don't have use of the full field, play across the width of the field with two PUGG style mini-goals evenly spaced on either side.

This game is all about transition from attacking to defending and vice-versa. When a team gains possession of the ball, they need to move quickly to support the teammate in possession. When a team loses possession, they need to transition quickly to defense and begin marking an **assigned** player. Practicing this skill will help your players understand their defensive responsibilities and apply these skills during restarts.

Pair players with comparable speed and ability to ensure even matchups. Players may only mark and tackle the opponent that they are assigned to! This will force players to cover their mark and anticipate/intercept passes. Reinforce the behavior of defending players being 'touch-tight' to their mark. This phrase means staying close enough to their target player so that they can literally reach out and touch them. The objective of this tight marking is to eliminate the passing options of the player with the ball.

Getting youth players to raise their voices and communicate can be one of the most challenging aspects of playing a smart game. Assign a team captain whose role it is to communicate (i.e., Yell) *"Support!"* or *"Mark-Up!"* depending upon whether they are gaining or losing possession. As is a universal law, whenever everybody is responsible for something, generally nobody does it. Therefore, assign individual responsibility to improve the behavior. Change the team captains after each goal.

Coaching Points:

- Encourage attackers to 'lose' their mark and get free to receive a pass. This is a great opportunity to also encourage supporting teammates to make ball-side runs around their teammate, who might be actively shielding, to receive a short layoff pass. This tactic is commonly referred to as 'overlapping' and is worthy of a short demonstration on the front-end of the drill. Set this up and communicate, "Lay it!" to your teammate as you overlap her.
- Anticipation – Players marking an opponent must not only keep up with that opponent, but they must also keep track of where the ball is and anticipate a pass to their mark. It's easy for players to pay so much attention to their mark and still get beat. Make sure that they are splitting their attention between their mark and the ball.

(10) Running w/ Cadence - There is a saying in soccer coaching that you should avoid the Three Evil L's of *"Lines, Laps, and Lectures"*, but running and conditioning are essential to being competitive. Be the leader of your pack (until you get one trained) and do a single lap around the field as the last part of this practice. Lead your pack with the following cadence and substitute your own club name/mascot where indicated. Do, however, stay away far away from 'Lines' and 'Lectures' as they consume precious time.

Caller: "Mama, Mama, can't you see?"
Pack: "Mama, Mama, can't you see?"
Caller: "What [Your Club] soccer's done to me!"
Pack: "What [Your Club] soccer's done to me!"
Caller: "I used to be a Princess...not any more!"
Pack: "I used to be a Princess...not any more!"
Caller: "I'm a soccer warrior knocking on your door!"
Pack: "I'm a soccer warrior knocking on your door!"
Caller: "Mama, Mama, can't you see?"
Pack: "Mama, Mama, can't you see?"
Caller: "What [Your Club] soccer's done to me?"
Pack: "What [Your Club] soccer's done to me?"
Caller: "My mind is strong and body is tough!"

Pack: "My mind is strong and body is tough!"
Caller: "We play like the devil and take no stuff!"
Pack: "We play like the devil and take no stuff!"
Caller: "Mama, Mama, can't you see?"
Pack: "Mama, Mama, can't you see?"
Caller: "What [Your Club] soccer's done to me?"
Pack: "What [Your Club] soccer's done to me?"
Caller: "I finally found what I wanna be!"
Pack: "I finally found what I wanna be!"
Caller: "I'm on [Mascot] team that cares about me!"
Pack: "I'm on [Mascot] team that cares about me!"
Caller: "Sound Off!"
Pack: "1, 2…"
Caller: "Sound Off!"
Pack: "3, 4…"
Caller: "What are we?!"
Pack: "Hard Core"
Caller: "Bring it on down"
Pack: "Hard core [Mascot]'s …Let's Go!"

Practice 5-2: Foot skills, sprints, 6v6 SSG unstructured

(25) Foot-Skills - Setup a General Foot Skills Practice Area according to diagram 1-1. Ensure that the first and last dribbling-lines in one row are spaced exactly 20 yards apart. These will be used for timing the sprints.

(5) Cone-to-cone dribble w/ Pull-Back Turn - Practice tight dribbling and then executing a pull-back turn with the same foot that was used for the dribble. Switch to the opposite foot for the pull-back and work on the non-dominant foot also. Remember to not let the foot touch the ground before taking a controlling touch on the ball.

(5) Static Step-Overs – This can be a challenging move to master for some players. While most players are starting to get it, there will be some that still needs work. So, we are going to keep it simple and continue to work on the basic mechanics of this fake. One common issue that prevents successful execution of this fake is NOT bringing the sweeping foot all the way back behind the ball so that the foot being used for the take-away has an unobstructed path to the ball. If the player simply steps short of the opposite side of the ball, she must then 'do a little dance' to perform the take away because the standing leg is now in the way. This adjustment destroys the move and compromises possession. Emphasize, heavily, this aspect of the move in the beginning of training.

(5) Dribble Side-to-Side w/ Step-Over – Use the inside of the foot to dribble cone-to-cone. Keep the ball close in front of the body while dribbling side-to-side as if screening a defender on the back. Dribble like you are 'screening' the ball from a defender that is trying to get it (See Practice 1-2). The hips should be facing perpendicular to the side-to-side dribble. Before getting to the cone, execute a step-over and change-of-direction and take the ball away with the inside of the foot. Do this in both directions.

(5) Step-Overs w/ Shadowing Defender – Same as the previous exercise, but have neighboring teammate apply passive pressure on the dribbler's back to simulate an active defender. Tell the neighboring teammate to leave their ball in-place and walk over to their teammate's space. Instruct the dribbler to look ('Check') over her shoulders periodically to track where the defender is. Simultaneously, have the shadowing defender stay low and keep their eyes riveted to the ball. This can be considered a secondary focus for defending.

(5) Figure 8s – Start with using the inside of the foot for cutting around the cones. Make sure that the players are crossing over in the middle to make 8s and not making Os. Graduate to using the outside of the foot to turn around cones. Add some stakes to the dribbling to get them to ramp-up their speed. Time how many they can do in a 60 second period and the last place dribbler has to run a big lap around the field. Watch them take-off when there are stakes involved. In the end, you don't have make the loser run, but explain to them that they need to practice like they are going to play, and that the speed they just dribbled at is 'game speed'.

(5) Hot Weather Water break

(25) Re-run Sprints to evaluate improvement. This will be the same configuration as was run in the previous practice but with a little progression. Ask them if they remember what good sprint form looks like. They will all most likely strike some type of pose that looks like what you are trying to accomplish. To illustrate what *not* to do, hold your arms in a manner that is incorrect and ask them, *"Does this look correct?"* For instance, hold the arms with everything good except for the elbows bent too far out. Or, clinch your fists while you are pumping your arms and see if they recognize the bad form. There are a lot of subtly incorrect ways you can get them to say "No" and make your point. Then show them the correct way and have them acknowledge the proper form.

The progression for this session is getting them to 'lean in' to their sprint and get their upper-torso past the vertical. Most players will already be doing this naturally, but some will be running in more of a straight up and down posture. I have even seen some players running with a 'leaning back' posture that absolutely saps their speed.

Add a little pressure by matching players up for a race, but each coach should still have a stopwatch to time them individually. Use the previously recorded times that should now be sorted on a spreadsheet...#1 runs with #2, #3 runs with #4, etc. Queue up lines on either side of the center cones so the players can better 'feel' each other's presence during the race. Emphasize to the runners that there is no benefit to turning your head and looking at the competitor. If you look to the side, you are losing speed and may lose the race. You should find the improvement over the previous weeks average times to be significant.

(5) Hot Weather Water break

(25) 2-Touch SSG - 6v6 on short field. The primary restriction being that players can take no more than two touches before they pass the ball to a teammate or take a shot on goal.

Progression: All players on the team in possession must be forward of the mid-field line, otherwise, any shot on goal doesn't count. If you take a shot and score without all players being forward, your team must do 5 pushups. If you score 'legally' then the other team must do 5 pushups.

Coaching Point: You have been training your players to take a safe touch into space for the last several weeks. Now it is time to start giving a 40 second time-out to any player that kicks the ball away to nowhere. Players hate being pulled out of the fun and it's also mildly embarrassing. If you really want to 'play it up' take a handful of red cones and create a 'Penalty Box' where the players will 'do their time'.   Going forward, push-ups and the 'penalty box' are a couple tools you can leverage to break this awful habit. The time-out is an effective tool in changing this behavior and I have seen results immediately. Now that your players have learned to take a 'touch into space', there is no excuse for them to give away possession anymore. Rather than put a stopwatch on them, have them just count to 40 using the honor system.

Practice 6-1: Wall-sprints, foot skills/dribbling, fake & finish, 6v6 SSG unstructured

(10) Wall-Sprints - Another simple tool that you can use to help your players run faster, without even running, are thigh-drives. Also known as 'wall sprints', thigh-drives against a wall can be used to improve form and strengthen hip flexors. The hip flexors are those groups of muscles (psoas major and rectus femoris) that run vertically across the hip and are directly responsible for raising the leg. The stronger these muscle groups, the more quickly the leg that has just pushed-off during the sprint can recover and drive forward. Hence, faster recovery from the push-off equals faster sprint performance.

I have been fortunate to have a building nearby with plenty of open wall surface to use for training. If you don't have a wall, an alternative training method is recommended at the end of this section. Have your players trot to the wall in preparation for the training...no walking...keep them moving.

*Figure 6-1: **Correct** Wall-Sprint Form*

Have your players gather around you for an explanation and demonstration of what they are going to do and why they are doing it. Lean on the wall with your arms outstretched (only slightly bent and parallel to the ground) so that your body is at about a 45-degree angle. The legs should be locked and you should be able to draw a straight line from head-to-heel (i.e., no bent body).

On the coach's command (*"Drive!"*), drive your left knee up almost parallel to the ground. It's important that this be a drive of the knee and not a swing of the leg to best replicate the motion of the sprint. The proper angle of the thigh is about 20 degrees from parallel to ground; See Figure 6-1 for an example of good form.   The knee should NOT be completely parallel to the ground or higher than the hip; See Figure 6-2 for an example of incorrect form. This driving action of the knee must be explosive to be effective and build strength. In this position, the toes should be pointed up toward the shin. Hold this position for about 5 seconds. Correct players that have not pulled their knee up high enough, have a bent body, or toes not pointed. Also, as with a regular sprint, the head should be up and facing directly forward.

On the coach's command (*"Drive!"*), Players explosively drive the locked knee forward and the raised leg backward just as if they were running. Repeat the pause and give corrections. Do this for about 10 repetitions and then let your players stand up and shake their legs up for a minute or so.

Put your players back against the wall and assume the 45-degree leaning position. Explain to them that they are going to do a 'double pump' starting with their left knee up. Instead of simply switching, they will drive the right knee and then back to the left (and hold) as quickly as they can. Hold for 5 seconds and then command "Drive!" for about 5 repetitions. Switch sides and repeat for the right leg.

IMPORTANT NOTE: The threshold of pain and tolerance for these times and repetitions will vary among your players. Pay close attention to your players that are struggling and adjust as necessary so as not to overwork them. It's also highly recommended that you research this topic and find some online video references to help guide you in delivering this training, there are loads of them out there.

Internet search phrase for finding these materials is: WALL SPRINT DRILL SPRINTING TECHNIQUE

Ask your players if they want to get faster. If they do, point out that they can do this exercise at home whenever they have a few extra minutes. It doesn't take loads time to get better, just a little bit each day. Encourage them to find a wall inside/outside their house that they can safely lean against. Tell them to be sure and wash their hands so that they don't leave hand prints and get in trouble with their parents!

*Figure 6-2: **Incorrect** Wall-Sprint Form*

(30) Foot Skills – Layout passing lanes 15 yards long and approximately 5 yards separation so that players are not on top of each other. See Figure 6-3 for details. Position 3 players per lane with two on one end and one on the other. Ball starts with the side that has two players.

(5) Messi-Style Dribbling w/Layoff - Dribble taking 'micro touches' on the ball with the instep, with every step. This training is inspired the by the legendary Barcelona player, Lionel Messi, with his ability to keep the ball just inches away from his feet at a full run. For introductory purposes, the pace of this training should be a slower dribble and is all about maintaining control. It's not a race to see who can get to the other side first.

Messi-Style Dribbling and Double Step-Over Progression

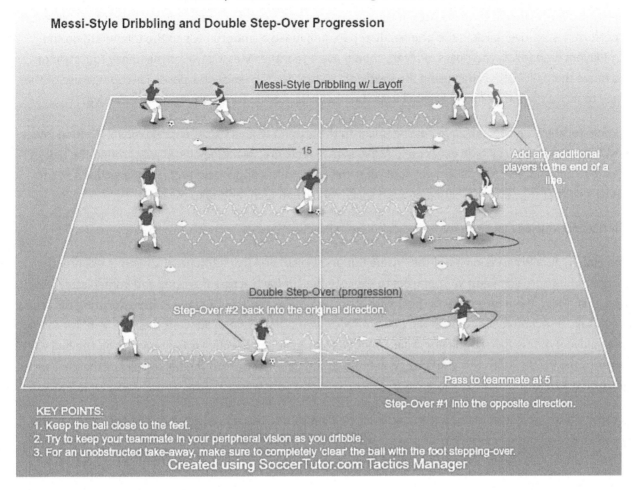

Figure 6-3

Instruct your players as they dribble that they should be over the ball in such a way that they can look nearly straight down and see the ball at their feet. The ball should never be more than 6" away from their dribbling foot. Their toes should be pointed down and the knees are raised slightly higher to achieve this manner of touch on the ball. Some players will tend to turn their feet in a little and dribble with the outside of their foot (pinky toe), just as you have been coaching previously. Correct this by telling them that 'pinky toe' is not incorrect, but just not the style of dribble that they are working on today. When the dribbler gets to the other side of the lane, she lays the ball off to her teammate who then dribbles to the other side.

The objective of training this style of dribble (with toes oriented down) is achieving tight fast ball control. In his analysis of Lionel Messi's dribbling style, Pablo Toledo of the soccer website The18.com succinctly describes the benefits of teaching this technique of tight dribbling. He states that, *"dribbling speed comes from our capacity to replicate the body motion of running without the ball."* (Toledo, 2020)

(5) Messi-Style Dribbling w/Layoff (progression) - Start training your players to look up and start paying attention to their teammate on the other side. Unless they are encouraged to get their heads up, they will be forever looking down on the ball. This little detail helps them to start improving their 'field awareness'. Encourage them to use their peripheral vision to keep both ball and teammate in their sight.

(10) Double Step-Overs - Dribble to the center of the lane, perform a step-over to change directions, dribble a few feet, then perform a step-over back in the original direction, and make a smooth pass to the teammate on the other side. Players then follow their pass. Players should use either the 'Messi' style or the 'pinky toe' style of dribbling to move the ball. Other than using the inside of the foot for take-away purposes, discourage use of the inside surface to move the ball. Moving the ball with the instep or outside foot is much more effective.

Coaching points for the step overs include getting lower to the ground when performing the move. Getting lower, as with most fakes, improves agility in execution. Make sure players are sweeping all the way around the ball so that they are leaving room for their take-away foot after the pivot in the opposite direction. If execution seems awkward, it's likely that they aren't creating enough space for a clean pivot and take-away.

(10) Outside/Outside/Inside Cut - Reference basic drill from Practice 1-1.

(20) Cut and Finish - Run Progression #3 of the 'Inside Cut and Finish' drill from Practice 1-2. This is a context-driven shooting drill where you want your players to execute the cut back across the body and immediately take their shot on goal. Have them target the far post with a shot on the ground immediately after executing the fake. If they have to take a second touch to push the ball out far enough, that's fine. You want them to 'aim' for the far post. As most players of this age are still not skilled enough to execute a perfectly straight pass/shot, the ball will generally veer to the inside. With this guidance, you hope to see balls rolling into the far corners of the goal and out of reach of the Keeper.

Put your Keepers in the goal to give them some practice fielding shots. The more they get to see in practice, the better they will perform during games. Your players, to this point, have been practicing these cuts almost every week (in some manner), so you will want to begin pushing them to move faster and take their shots quicker.

As with the criss-cross finishing that you do in the pre-game warm-up, have your assistant coach in the goal to feed out a 2nd ball to simulate the Goal Keeper slapping down or otherwise bobbling a save (rebounding) back into the playing area. **TRAIN YOUR PLAYERS TO HUNT FOR REBOUNDS!** This is an undertrained skill in developing attackers in soccer. Every shot taken within the goal area should be followed up on. Get your players into the mindset that the shot on goal is also the first step in the sprint for any potential rebound.

Coaching Points:

- Take great pains to let them know that it's better to shoot and barely miss wide than it is to kick the ball straight to the Goal Keeper. Keep drilling it into their heads that, *"The Goal Keeper is NOT your friend. Don't give her any 'presents' to improve her confidence and make her look good in front of her team, coach, and parents."* It takes a lot of work hard work on everyone's part to get the ball into the goal area…don't give the ball away.
- It's amazing how many players (recreational *and* club), can lift the ball up and over the cross-bar from the penalty spot. Keep drilling them to keep the ball on the ground. Do this by striking the middle of the ball instead of underneath it. Do this by getting their kicking knee over the top of the ball as they strike.

(30) 6v6 SSG w/ Kick-Off Restart - Reference basic drill from Practice 4-2. Encourage wingers to mark their counterparts on kick-offs and encourage good general marking when out-of-possession. Have a ball ready for a quick kick-off each time a goal is scored. Remember to enforce the 40 second time-out for a kick-away. This is the most powerful tool in your box for training control and possession.

Practice 6-2: Strength, sprints, foot skills, directional 1st-touch, 3v3, and tug-o-war

(10) High Stepping - This technique of strengthening the hip flexors is an alternative to doing the Thigh-Drives against a wall. Understandably, not everyone has a wall available, so these exercises can be done right on the field. As with the thigh-drives, all players can do these at the same time.

Layout a cone-line about 15 yards from one of the marked lines on the field. This will be the point to which the high-stepping will occur. Spread your players out arms width from each other on the marked line. With hands on hips, raise up on the balls of the feet and start high-stepping to the cone-line. The knees should higher than the hip (i.e., not level). DO NOT come off of the balls of the feet while stepping; By design, this exercise also strengthens the ankles. Upon reaching the cone-line, turn around and jog back to the other side. Do 2 sets of this basic high-stepping.

Progression: Do 2 sets of high-stepping that incorporate a pause where players briefly hold their leg up, similar to the thigh-drives taught in practice 6-1. Players must place their heels on the ground for this exercise and should hold their hands out to their sides for balance. Light jog back to the starting point when finished.

The next 2 sets of high-stepping incorporate the arm-pumps that you instructed in practice 5-1. Step briskly to the cone-line while coordinating the arm-swing with the knee raises. This might look a little funny and robotic, but is great context training to developing good running form.

As with the Thigh-Drives, explain to your players that they can do these exercises at home if they really want to get faster.

(15) Re-run Sprints to Evaluate Improvement – Same training as in Week 5-2. This session is 10 minutes shorter than before, so you will only be able to run each player about 2-3 times tops. Be sure to continue recording times to measure improvement. Do your best to watch players individually and give meaningful feedback.

(30) Foot Skills – Run the same foot skills session as in Week 6-1.

(15) Passing around a square – Reference basic drill from Practice 4-1.

(20) 3v3 Tournament on mini goals – 3v3 continuous play on 2 fields 15x30 yards. Place one mini-goal at the long end of each field. Watch for goal guarding and give anyone that does it a 40 second time-out. Keep track of goals, and after 10 minutes, have the winners play each other. Coaches should have extra balls in-hand in case the active ball is kicked out of play.

(5) Tug-O-War - Just because we can. One of the underlying objectives of this overall training plan is to increase the assertiveness of your players, particularly for girls as they tend to be more reserved. There is nothing so good as a tug-o-war to 'release the beast' within every player. Subconsciously, every little activity like this serves to foster that spirit of assertiveness in your players.

Consider getting a multi-purpose length of rope for this and the jump rope activity. I think the perfect rope for jumping and tugging (both on grass) is an All-Purpose UnManila Polypropylene style construction of 5/8" diameter and 50 ft. in length. 50' ft. is perfect for tugging, but too long for jumping, so you and your assistant coach will have to 'choke up' on the line to a manageable length for swinging.

Setting up a tug-o-war is simple. Set out two cones about 6 feet apart. Evenly space the rope across these two cones and tie-off a pinnie in the middle. When the teams tug, the winner is determined when the pinnie is pulled across one of the cones.

Players, and people in-general, like to be empowered. So, select two of your players of smaller stature to be captains and empower them to pick teams. Flip a coin to see who gets first pick and watch the fun begin. When you do this, it doesn't end up being a case where the smaller players are always picked last and have to deal with the stigma of appearing weak.

If you opt to not do a Tug-O-War, just add the extra 5 minutes on to the 3v3 tournament and swap teams after 12 minutes instead of 10.

Practice 7-1: Foot skills, directional 1st-touch, 4v4+4N possession, 6v6 SSG unstructured

(15) Foot Skills - Setup a General Foot Skills Practice Area according to diagram 1-1.

(5) Cuts Behind Standing Leg - This fake is used to evade defenders and change direction away from pressure. Demonstrate the skill on-the-move. Slow it down if necessary and perform without dribbling. If you are unfamiliar with the skill, you search the terms SOCCER CUT BEHIND LEG (CRYUFF) to find a number of good examples.

(5) Side-to-Side Step-Overs - Move side-to-side between cones with hips facing perpendicular to the direction of dribble. Reiterate that the ball should always be directly in front of them and they should be using controlled touches with the inside of their foot. Quickly progress to having their neighbor 'shadow' them from side-to-side on their back as you only have few minutes. As before, have the dribbler turn their head just enough to keep track of where the defender is. Switch roles to allow the 'shadowing defender' to dribble some.

(5) Figure 8s - Similar to what was performed in previous practices. Have players start by cutting around the cones with the inside of their foot. Each turn around the cone should be accomplished with 2-3 small 'cuts' before taking away in the opposite direction. Make sure player are crossing in the middle and using the outside of their foot (or their instep; whichever they prefer) to dribble to the other side.

After a couple of minutes, switch to using the outside of the foot to cut around the cones. When practicing using the outside of the foot to perform the cut, they should not be using the inside of their foot for any reason. To add a little bit of pressure and get them moving faster, visit each player and tell them, *"I'm after your ball!"* Chase them with light pressure as they cut around the cone and turn in the opposite direction. You want to get them moving and cutting at progressively faster speeds. If you don't add some type of pressure to the drill it will end-up being executed at a sub-optimal pace.

(15) Passing around a square - Reference basic drill from Practice 4-1.

(30) 4v4+4N Possession - Getting players to utilize support offered by their teammates is a challenge all the way up to high school levels of competition. This drill is all about taking advantage of support to protect the ball. It's nothing more than a big game of 'keep away' to see which team can complete the highest number of consecutive passes amongst themselves in a given period of time.

Layout a grid 20 x 20 paces without any goals according to Figure 7-1. Divide the players up into 3 teams and give them orange, blue, and green pinnies (or whatever colors you have). A team of 12 players divides perfectly into the 4v4+4 configuration, but that is rarely the case. So, don't worry if you have the odd player(s), just assign them to one team or the other and play on.

4v4 +4 Neutral - Possession

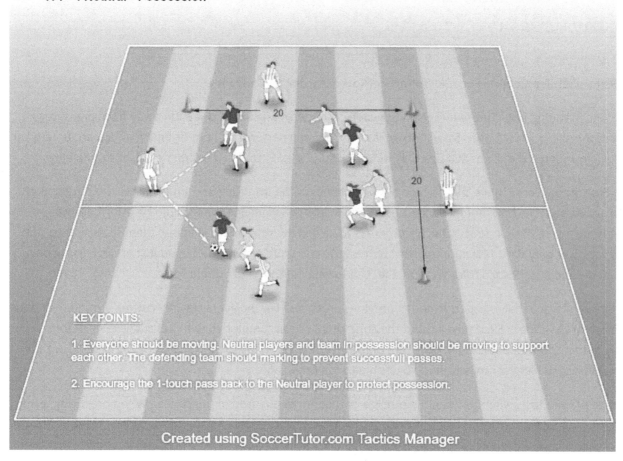

Figure 7-1

Orange and blue will start in the middle and compete for possession. Position one green player on each side of the square to serve as a neutral player. Two greens can occupy one side if you have an extra player. The neutral players (outside) are options for the team in possession. These neutral players cannot pass to neutral players on the other sides and they cannot enter the square at any time.

The coach starts the play by simply passing to one team or the other in the middle. Make sure someone is counting the number of consecutive passes and keeping up with who has the record. Encourage players to pass back to each other if it makes sense to keep possession of the ball. Encourage players to spread out, make themselves available (support), and call for the ball. Run each game for 2 minutes and then substitute-in the neutral players.

Coaching Points:

- There should be a lot of movement during this drill. Teammates should be moving to a position of support to be able to receive a pass from the player on the ball.
- Encourage players on the ball to be strong, and shield if necessary, until passing options are available.
- Encourage the players on the outside to one-touch pass back to players on the inside.
- Let them know it's OK to pass straight back to a player they just received a pass from. This often happens in a game when defenders chase the ball.

Be vocal during the game and give loads of praise and corrections to players that deserve and need it.

(30) 6v6 SSG Unstructured – Reference basic drill from Practice 3-1. Remember to enforce the 40 second time-out for a kick-away. This is the most powerful tool in your box for training control and possession.

Practice 7-2: Speed & agility, foot skills, shuffle passing, bullseye soccer, and giant soccer

(10) Wall Sprints - See basic drill from Practice 6-1. Lengthen or add an additional set as you see fit, but make sure that you don't wear them out.

(10) Ankle Hops - Layout a couple of 15 Ft. sections of a good speed/agility ladder for your players to do ankle hops through. By 'good' ladder, I mean one that DOES NOT have adjustable slats. When one of your not-so-graceful players snags the ladder during her run, these slats will slide and the whole ladder gets pulled out of alignment. Having a ladder with non-adjustable slats will allow you to simply grab the ends and quickly pull the whole ladder straight again.

If you don't have an agility ladder, you can simply use cones for your players to 'hop over' and work their ankles. Ladders are nice in that they provide a well-defined space for your players to step in and around. Don't overestimate the element of 'fun' that an agility ladder will add to your training. It is most likely that none of your youth players will have stepped through an agility ladder and it will be something that they look forward to.

Gather your players around and demonstrate what you want them to do. It's pretty simple, keep your legs close together, get up on the balls of your feet, and begin hopping through the rungs. Heels MUST NOT touch the ground during the hop. You should have a queue of 6-7 players on the end of each ladder-set. Tell them to begin and instruct the next person in line to begin hopping when the person in-front of them reaches the 4th rung.

The ankle hop is just one of many creative speed/strength/agility exercises you can do with an agility ladder. The following simple Internet search can provide you with many different options: AGILITY LADDER DRILLS FOR FASTER FOOTWORK

If you really want to add an element of fun (and pressure) to this drill, have them hang a pinnie out of the back of their shorts and tell them that they can stop if they capture the pinnie of the player in front of them. If you do this challenge, I highly recommend that you use cones instead of a ladder. Make sure the next player doesn't start too soon so that it remains a challenge.

(20) Foot Skills – Setup a General Foot Skills Practice Area according to diagram 1-1. The Giant Tick-Tocks and Chops will be done through the long channels.

(5) Messi Dribbling w/Layoff – Same basic drill as found in section 7-2, but from the beginning, ensure that your players are getting their heads up and looking at their teammates toward whom they are dribbling. Instruct them to look up enough so that they can see both the ball and their teammate at the same time. It's not a case of looking at one or the other; train for peripheral vision of both ball and field to avoid approaching defenders. Being the 2nd or 3rd time that your players have done this drill, push them to be a little faster than they have before.

(5) Double Step-Over w/pass – From a forward dribble, players execute a 180 degree change of direction with a step-over, take a light controlling touch away with the *inside* of the foot, and then immediately perform the same move back in the original direction followed with a firm pass to their teammate on the other side. The receiving player controls the ball and performs the same skill-move to the other side. The player making the pass *sprints* to

the back of the line. Players waiting to receive the ball need to be up on the balls of their feet (agile w/knees bent) so that they can be ready to receive the ball with either foot.

(5) Giant Tick-Tocks - This is an oversized tick-tock movement with forward motion as a precursor to training the Andres Iniesta (FC Barcelona) style 'La Croqueta' fake. This action is more of a 'sliding' motion of the ball from one side to the other, rather than striking the ball. To gain a little more context, you may want to research the La Croqueta fake using the Internet references in section 10-2.

Exactly as in the Inside Cuts drill in Practice 5-1, have your players queue up at the ends of the long channel and send them down individually with enough spacing that they don't run over the top of each other. Down one channel and back up the other…keep them moving.

(5) Inside Cuts on the Move - Reference basic drill from Practice 5-1. Start pushing your players to dribble faster and tighter and execute the chop with just enough force to beat the defender but still maintain control. At some point the speed of execution has to be feverish to beat a defender; eventually, anything less than game-speed will result in the defender being able to effectively anticipate and respond to the fake.

(10) Shuffle Passing - This is an elementary exercise is designed to train one-touch passing on an angle and movement to support. Most players are conditioned to stopping the ball during receiving and then making their pass. These passes are most often linear back to their teammate when practicing. This behavior greatly slows down the game and makes it much easier for a competitor to close-down your players and compete for the ball. Shuffle passing is one of those drills that trains a mindset of keeping the ball in motion (one-touch) and prepares your players for setting up 2v1 situations to beat defenders.

Lay out two stations according to Figure 7-2 and you can keep most of your players moving and avoid downtime. Set two lines of 10 cones spaced two paces apart, offset to each other with 2 paces of separation. This will essentially look like a zig-zag pattern.

In pairs, players will one-touch pass to each other through the cones and move to receive the next pass. One-touch is the goal, but if they have to do 2-touch for control, that's OK. They should be facing square to each other and 'shuffle' to the next opening to receive a pass. This means that their legs should not cross while they are moving. With this being a relatively new skill (one-touch on an angle), speed isn't necessarily the objective in the beginning. The goal should be to keep the ball moving accurately and to hustle in the next supporting position.

This is an easy drill for players to run over the top of each other, so start the next pair passing as soon as the current pair reaches the mid-point. Have your assistant coach manage the 2nd station. If you are lucky enough to a 3rd coach, have her manage a third station if you have enough cones. When players exit the third station, have them dribble back to the beginning of the 1st station.

Progressions: For the first 5 minutes, everyone uses their left foot for passing. The last 5 minutes, everyone uses their right foot. This makes managing stations uncomplicated.

Coaching Points:

- Slow it down just enough to maintain control
- Easy touch…it doesn't take much force to pass over this short distance

- Be sure to use inside of the foot for now. Some will use the outside of the foot, which is not wrong, but just not what we are training right now.
- As a matter of encouraging communication, get players talking to each other through drill.

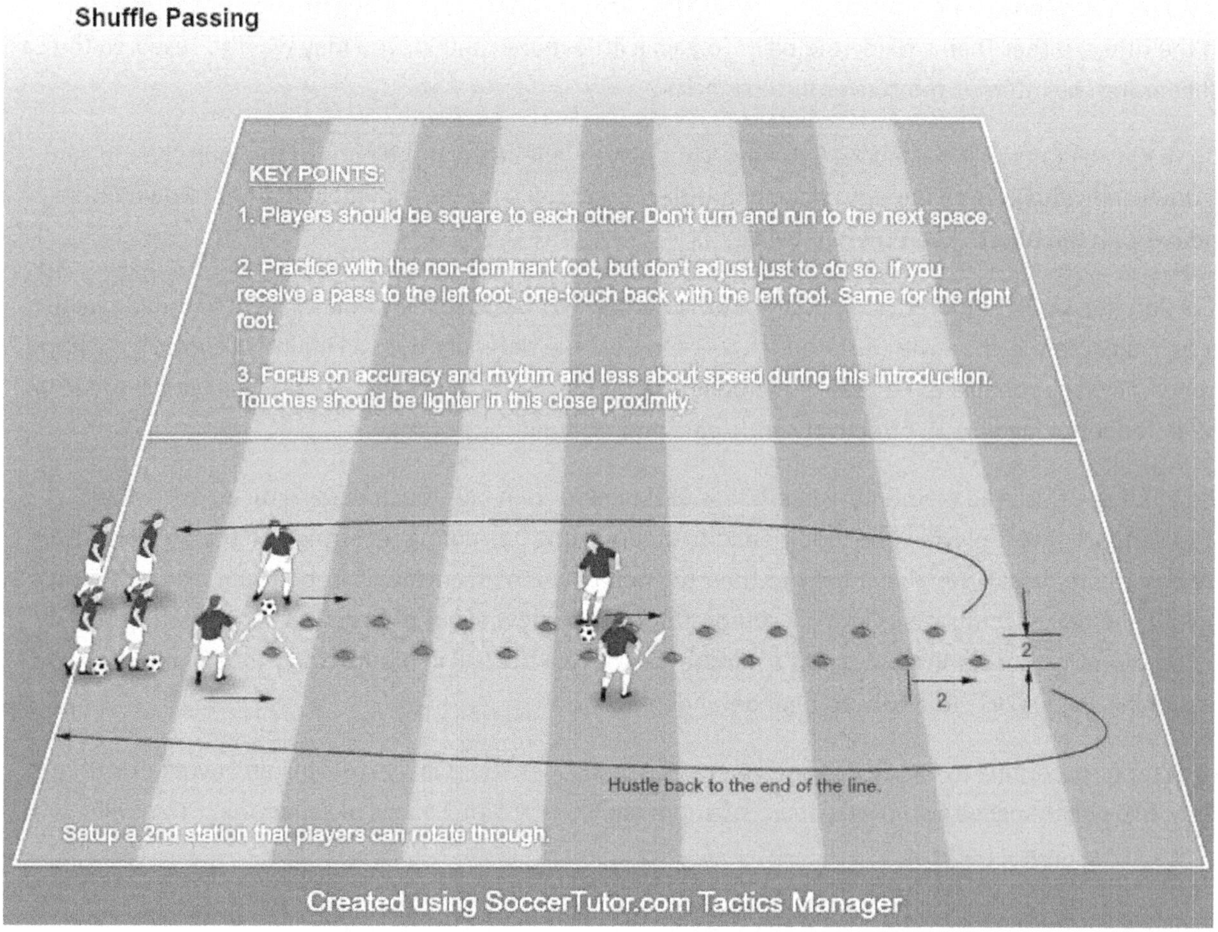

Shuffle Passing

KEY POINTS:

1. Players should be square to each other. Don't turn and run to the next space.

2. Practice with the non-dominant foot, but don't adjust just to do so. If you receive a pass to the left foot, one-touch back with the left foot. Same for the right foot.

3. Focus on accuracy and rhythm and less about speed during this introduction. Touches should be lighter in this close proximity.

Hustle back to the end of the line.

Setup a 2nd station that players can rotate through.

Created using SoccerTutor.com Tactics Manager

Figure 7-2

(20) Bulls Eye Soccer – This is a fun passing/interception game that pits three teams of 4 against each other yet requires cooperation between two teams attacking.

Layout a *single* target-style playing area as indicated in Figure 7-3. Players in the center will be Targets, players in the middle layer will be Defenders, and players on the outside will be Shooters. The objective is for the Shooters to get around the Defender and make successful passes on the ground to the Targets. Conversely, it is the objective of the Defenders to prevent successful passes. This exercise teaches the center players to show/communicate for the ball and make themselves available. It teaches the middle players to mark opponents and intercept passes, and it teaches the Attackers to lose their mark and find windows-of-opportunity to make their passes.

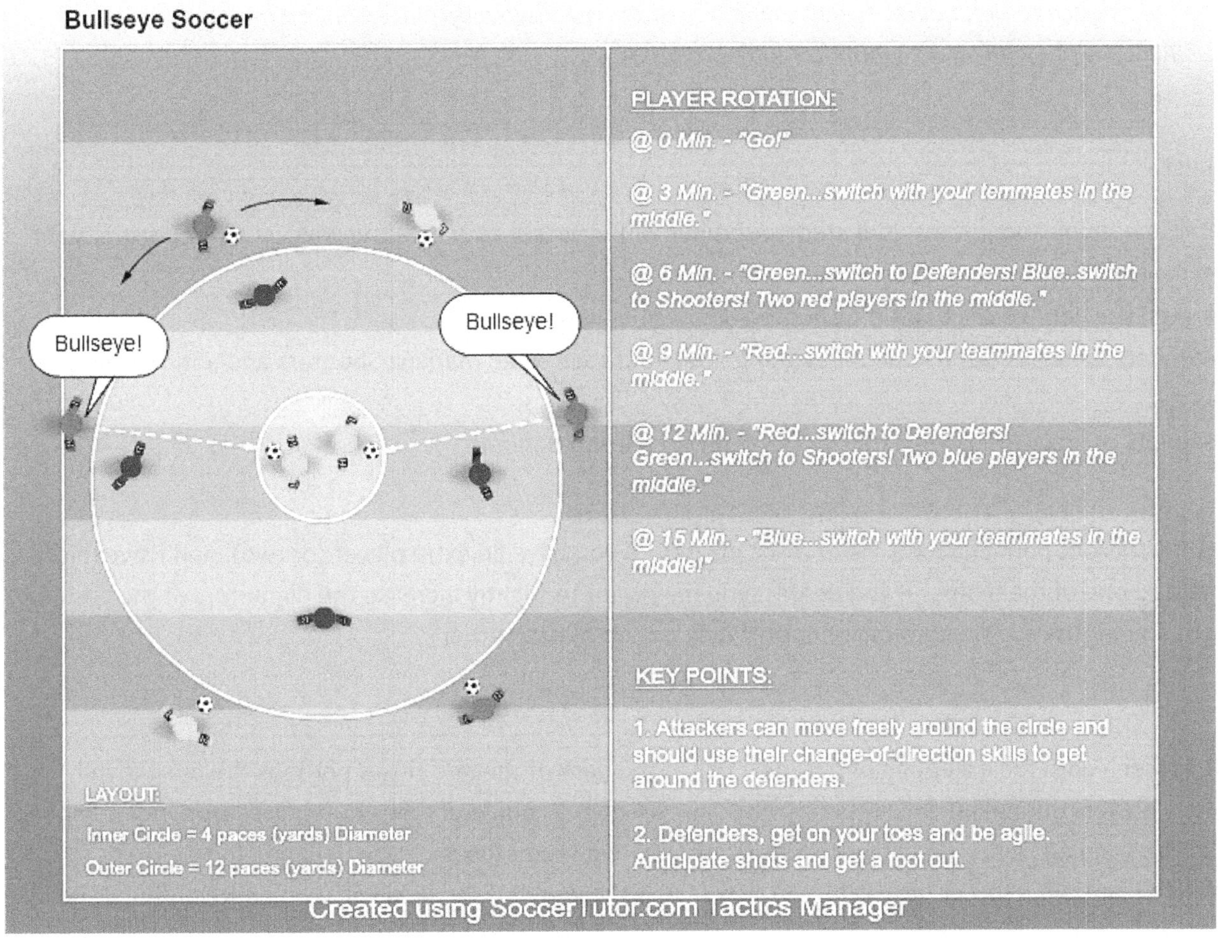

Bullseye Soccer

Figure 7-3

Time-management is your friend. Have the practice ready to go by pre-positioning pinnies as indicated in the diagram. 20 minutes isn't a lot of time and you want everyone to have a chance to be a Target; to do this, you must be organized.

Maximize your time by having them wear one of the pinnies you have laid out and remain in that spot. Do this as they are coming back from a quick drink or transition directly from Shuffle Passing if they are not overworked. This buys you critical time to deliver instructions while they are putting on pinnies. From the beginning, keep the energy level up and keep them moving.

Bark out, *"Alright, time to play Bulls Eye Soccer, everyone put on a pinnie and remain in that spot!"*

Take just a couple of minutes to explain/demonstrate the exercise and incorporate the coaching points mentioned in the paragraph above. Have them yell "Bulls Eye!" if they make a successful pass to a Target player.

After instruction, set the game in motion with the following fast timeline:

@ 00:00   *"Go!"*
@ 03:00   *"Green…switch with your teammates in the middle!"*
@ 06:00   *"Green…switch to Defenders! Blue…switch to Shooters! Two red players in the middle!"*
@ 09:00   *"Red…switch with your teammates in the middle!"*

@ 12:00   *"Red...switch to Defenders! Green...switch to Shooters! Two blue players in the middle!"*
@ 15:00   *"Blue...switch with your teammates in the middle!"*

Coaching points:

- Attackers, think about using your step-over move or lunge fake to create the window-of-opportunity for the pass.
- Targets, use your voices to let the Shooters know you are available.
- Defenders, be agile! Bend your knees and get on your toes when marking Shooters and anticipating passes.
- Heap lots of praise on players that successfully attack and defend!

This exercise works out perfectly for a roster of 12 players. If you have an extra player (or two), don't sweat it. Just add them to one of the teams. If you do this, you may want to slightly increase the diameters of the circles by an extra yard so that the middle players are not running on top of each other.

(20) Giant Soccer - With the exception of putting a ball in the back of the net, this is perhaps the most joyful activity for my players during the entire season. I usually try do it a couple of times during a season, but it appears only once in this training plan. This activity is simply turning two teams loose on the field and letting them compete with a giant (40") soccer ball. Let them play across the width of the field with the entire end-lines being the goal.

Make sure you get an appropriate ball. The one I use is sold under the brand of Everrich™. At the time of this writing, you can find this ball on www.AthleticStuff.com by searching on GIANT 40" SPORTS BALLS. It's a very durable ball with a heavy-duty PVC bladder and cloth outer cover and can withstand a lot of abuse. Another reason for using the 40" ball vs. anything larger is that it's ready to go. You can inflate the Everrich™ 40" ball and still fit it into the back of an SUV...ready to be unveiled toward the end of practice. Be advised that you will need a heavy-duty air pump to inflate this ball to its full glory. The tiny pumps used to inflate the typical air mattresses are simply insufficient.

Another thing that I like to do to 'gin-up' the fun during this, and other fun exercises, is to play some high-energy music. More recently, I've purchased a 100W portable speaker that connects with my phone via Bluetooth. Before that, I simply put together music on a CD and played if from my car with the doors and hatch open.

These are my selections for anyone looking for a shortcut to a high-energy playlist:

Mama Said Knock You Out   by   LL Cool J
Get Down Tonight   by   KC and the Sunshine Band
Gonna Make You Sweat   by   C+C Music Factory
Hey Ya   by   Outkast
Don't Stop Til You Get Enough   by Michael Jackson
Shake It Off   by   Taylor Swift

Uptown Funk   by   Bruno Mars
Runnin' Down a Dream   by   Tom Petty
Welcome to the Jungle   by   Guns-n-Roses
California Love   by   2PAC w/ Dr. Dre
Animals   by   Maroon 5
Lonely Boy   by   The Black Keys

Unfortunately, these oversized balls aren't cheap; they run about $85 apiece and can be cost prohibitive for some. If you are unable to splurge for this specialized equipment, you might consider substituting a fun game of 'World Cup' for this last 20 minutes of training. If you are unfamiliar with this game, do a simple Internet search on the terms 'FUN WORLD CUP SOCCER DRILL' to find plenty of good references.

Practice 8-1: Foot skills, sprints, dribbling circuit, shuffle passing, and 6v6 SSG unstructured

Layout the multi-purpose field indicated in Practice 1-1. Additionally, you will want to have already laid out a couple of 'Cross Roads Dibbling' and 'Shuffle Passing' stations as the schedule for this session will be tight.

(25) Foot Skills – The purpose of this session is to use the step-over move to turn the ball into the attacking direction with a defender on the back. This is a circumstance that players can find themselves in most anywhere on the field, but you are going to teach it within an attacking context. If you have followed this training regiment, you have already taught your players the important first-step of being 'strong on the ball' through Shielding. Now you get teach them a bit of self-reliance in attacking in-order to move the ball forward.

(10) Step-Over and take-away w/ outside of foot – At this point, your players will have developed reasonably good form in executing the basic Step-Over. Though some will have inadvertently begun using the outside of their foot to take the ball away, this is where we begin in earnest using that surface of the foot to extend their skills.

(5/10) Step-Over w/ simple take-away: Start your players centered on the ball and between the two cones at their station. Take a position with your back to your players and demonstrate the technique as they would perform it. On your command of *"Go!"*, have them, in unison, explosively 'sweep' the ball like they normally do, but this time take-away in the opposite direction with the outside of their foot. Having them all perform the skill at the same time, and then resetting, helps you identify players that are having difficulty. Make sure they don't take the ball away too hard, but keep it tight to the foot so as not to risk losing it to a nearby defender. Work on this basic skill for about 5 minutes alternating feet.

(5/10) Step-Over w/ angled take-away: After 5 minutes, you want to progress to a more 'hooking' motion of pulling the ball behind the back in the opposite direction (toward the goal!). This is the 'bread and butter' part of the move that is designed to turn with a defender on the back. Instead of simply taking a touch in the opposite direction, use the outside of the foot to curl around the front of the ball and pull it behind at an angle of approximately 45 degrees. Demonstrate what you want them to do so that they know what good execution looks like. You also want them getting into the habit of raising their arm to help fight off a defender that adjusts quickly. For their entire lives, most youngsters have been conditioned to respect personal space and to not push and shove; Start re-programming your players that it is OK to use arms and hands when battling-for and protecting the ball. Practice this move with both feet and work on getting their 45-degree angle of take-away correct.

(15) Turn w/ Shadowing Defender: This segment of training adds an element of reality with the addition of a passive defender. Instruct the players in every other row to leave their ball where it is and step forward to approximately arms-length from their neighbor's back. Have them get into a proper side-on position that is characteristic of a traditional 'close down' and adjust their distance by putting their fingertips on the attacker's middle back. This is as close as you want your players to be when defending at an attacker's back. Being too tight on the back is a classic mistake that allows the attacker to 'spin-off' the defender and move in the direction of your goal. As the attacker moves side-to-side in preparation for her step-over fake, the defender should adjust to this movement by quickly switching lead legs to be facing the direction the ball is moving. This is the extent to which you want the shadowing defender to participate; you want them to be low, fast, and agile in tracking the ball. For training purposes only, you do *not* want them challenging for the ball when the attacker makes her turn.

Demonstrate once or twice so that your players can see how both roles are properly executed then set them in-motion to practice at their own pace.

Coaching Points:

- Emphasize the 45-degree angle of take-away. The goal is to turn around the defender rather than simply take the ball away 'square' (to the side).
- Push for speed of execution, no defender will be fooled by a move that is executed at a leisurely pace.
- DO NOT strike the ball, but rather 'pull/guide' it back in a smooth and controlled fashion. You shouldn't hear a 'thud' during the take-away. The movement should be one fluid motion where the dribbler turns and pulls/pushes the ball into space.
- Make your rounds and heap plenty of praise on those making progress and offer individual instruction to those that need a little more help.

While this is something of a 'two birds with one stone' type of drill with guidance to the defender, remember that this is primarily an 'attacking focused' drill, so that's where you want to keep your emphasis with respect to attention and corrections. 75% (or more) of corrections should be focused on proper execution of the Step-Over and 25% (or less) on defensive jockeying.

(15) Sprints (20 yard) – If you want to get better at something, you got to practice at it. It's not enough to just show your players how to run, they must continue to practice at it in order to get better. As before, line your players up into two competing queues, and matching up players according to closest time. For this set of sprints, lose the stopwatch and simply watch them closely and give constructive feedback on their sprint form. By this time in the season, I've found that many players really want to get faster. I've even had parents tell me that their kids are practicing sprinting at home.

(15) Crossroads Dribbling – This is another timed personal-challenge style drill that players love to do. Following Figure 8-1, lay out 5 coaching sticks (or cones) in the shape of a 'plus' sign with the 4 outer poles being 7 adult paces from the center. You don't need coaching sticks to run this drill, but they are a much more effective obstacle for enforcing the turns.

Crossroads Dribbling

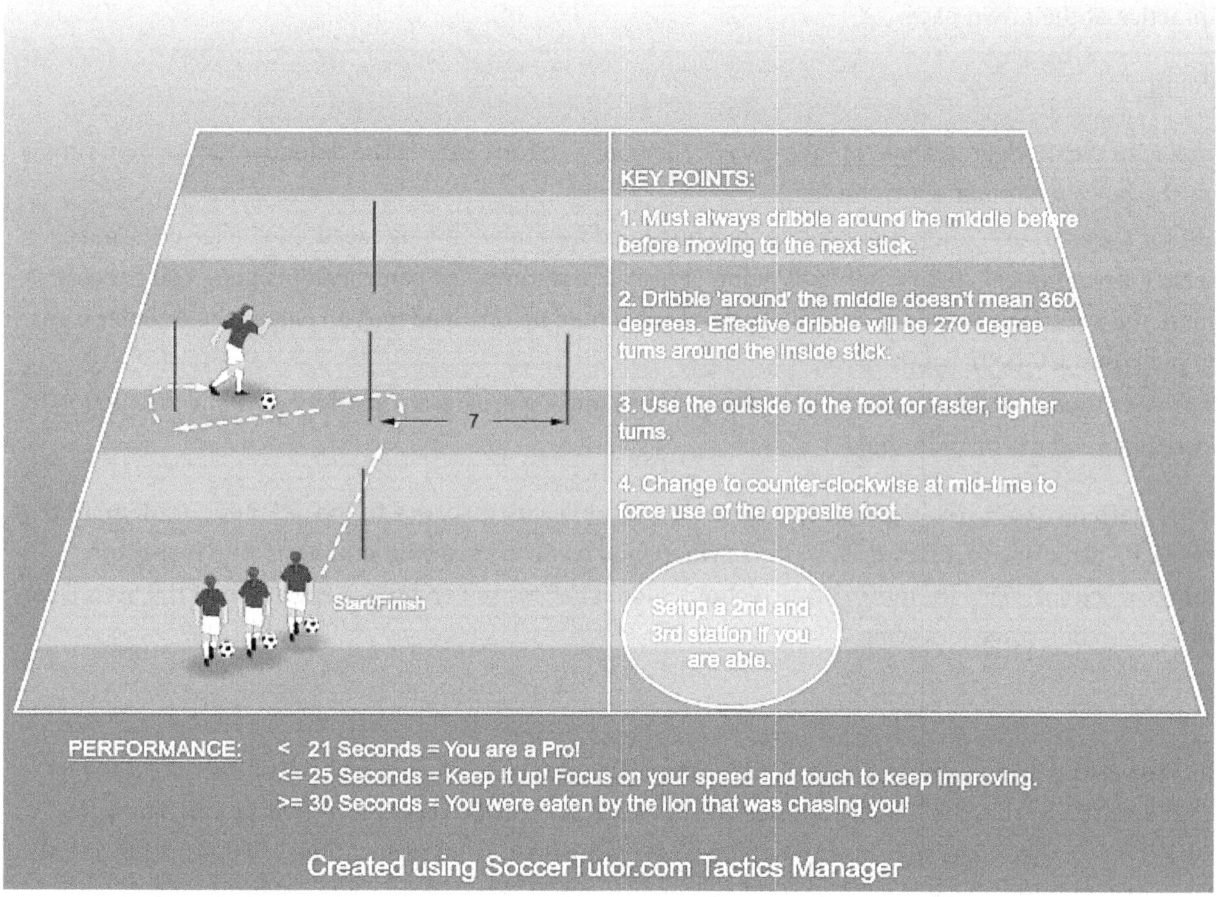

KEY POINTS:

1. Must always dribble around the middle before before moving to the next stick.

2. Dribble 'around' the middle doesn't mean 360 degrees. Effective dribble will be 270 degree turns around the inside stick.

3. Use the outside fo the foot for faster, tighter turns.

4. Change to counter-clockwise at mid-time to force use of the opposite foot.

Setup a 2nd and 3rd station if you are able.

7

Start/Finish

PERFORMANCE: < 21 Seconds = You are a Pro!
<= 25 Seconds = Keep it up! Focus on your speed and touch to keep improving.
>= 30 Seconds = You were eaten by the lion that was chasing you!

Created using SoccerTutor.com Tactics Manager

Figure 8-1

The objective is for the individual dribbler to start at one pole and dribble clockwise around each of the outside sticks. The dribbler must dribble around the middle stick to get to the next outside stick. Players can use either surface of their foot to dribble around the poles as quickly as they can. Keep it simple and have players dribble in a clockwise or counter-clockwise direction (their choice). The player must be in possession of the ball when dribbling past the last post. Watch for some of your more creative players to kick their ball past the last pole while trying to improve their time.

For a group of 11-year-old players, these are some expected times: Fastest = 20.6 seconds, Average = 24.7 seconds, and Slowest = 30.1 seconds.

Coaching Points (for faster times):

- Fewer touches = faster times! If you can take a slightly heavier (and still accurate) touch in the direction of the next pole, do so. Otherwise, simply keep the ball tight to your feet and move as quickly as you can.
- Make sure you take your touch to the correct side of the center pole so that you don't have to dribble 360 degrees around it on your way to the next pole in the sequence.
- Use the outside of your foot to turn around the poles. Using the outside of the foot allows you to turn tighter and eliminate extra touches.

(10) Shuffle Passing – Same basic drill as instructed in practice 7-2. Continue working on controlled 1-2 touch passes on an angle.

(25) 6v6 SSG w/ Glow Ball - Run this game on a short field similar to past practices. If you are delivering this training in the Fall, it's probably starting to get dark toward the end of your practices. An element of this training that has always been well-received (and fun) is the use of the glow ball. It will eventually get so dark that the only thing you will be able to see is the ball rolling across the ground, yet your players will still be calling to each other for passes!

You can easily find the ball that I use on Amazon with the following search term: **Kan Jam Illuminate Ultra-Bright LED Light-Up Glow Soccer Ball, Size 5**

Coaching Point: In the midst of all the fun that is being had, remember to be the 'bad guy' and enforce the 40 second time-out for a kick-away. This is the most powerful tool in your box for training control and possession.

Practice 8-2: Jump rope, foot skills, turning (defender on back), 4v4+4N, 6v6 SSG unstructured

(10) Jump Rope (warm up) - On the surface, this may seem a completely unproductive activity, but don't underestimate the benefits. This activity strengthens the ankles not unlike the 'ankle hops' that you did in a previous training session. Jumping rope offers yet another valuable conditioning tool, and at the same time, elevates your reputation as a coach that makes training fun.

If you begged, borrowed, stole, or bought the rope referenced for use in the tug-o-war, well done! You and your players are going to have a great time. The 5/8" x 50' is going to be too long for jumping, so you and your assistant coach will have to 'choke up' on the line to a manageable length for swinging.

It's so easy, even if you haven't done it before. You and your assistant coach just need to start swinging and your players will run into the swinging rope one at a time until one of the jumpers trips the rope.

You can find loads of experts extolling the health benefits of jumping rope by using the following Internet search phrase: JUMPING ROPE HELPS WITH SPRINTING

(20) Foot Skills - Layout the multi-purpose field indicated in Practice 1-1.

(5) Messi-style Dribbling – Reference basic drill from Practice 7-2.

(5) Double Step-Over w/pass – Reference basic drill from Practice 7-2.

(5) Step-Over w/ angled take-away – Same drill as from Practice 8-1. Take-away at 45-degrees behind with the outside of the foot. Alternate feet. This is in preparation for the 1v1 drill to train turning with a defender on the back.

(5) Giant Tick-Tocks – Reference basic drill from Practice 7-2.

(20) 1v1 Defender on Back – This drill serves to create a game-like context where an attacker receives the ball in the penalty area with a defender on her back and she must turn the ball toward the goal to get a shot off quickly. This drill is conducted with light-to-moderate pressure on the attacker so that she can experience some success executing the Step-Over fake that she has been training.

Following Figure 8-2, place a small cone between the penalty spot and the top of the 18-yard box. This is where the attacker will be positioned facing the top of the 18-yard box from where the coach will serve the ball. Position a defender about two steps back from the attacker facing in the same direction. The defender can engage as soon as the ball is played into the attacker.

1v1 Defender on Back

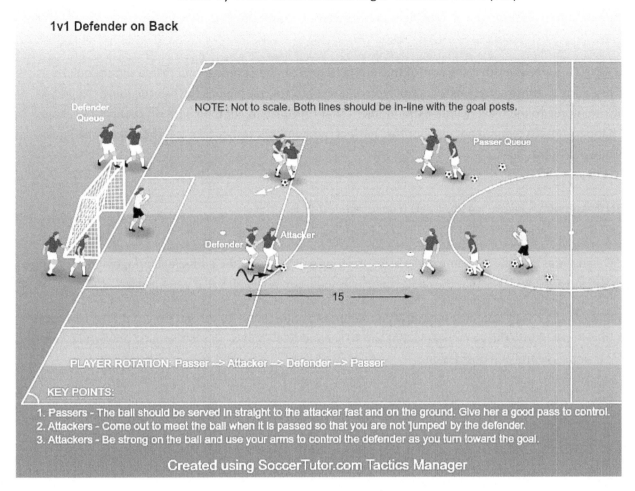

NOTE: Not to scale. Both lines should be in-line with the goal posts.

Defender Queue

Passer Queue

Attacker

Defender

15

PLAYER ROTATION: Passer --> Attacker --> Defender --> Passer

KEY POINTS:

1. Passers - The ball should be served in straight to the attacker fast and on the ground. Give her a good pass to control.
2. Attackers - Come out to meet the ball when it is passed so that you are not 'jumped' by the defender.
3. Attackers - Be strong on the ball and use your arms to control the defender as you turn toward the goal.

Created using SoccerTutor.com Tactics Manager

Figure 8-2

Use this drill to encourage verbal and non-verbal communication between attacking teammates. To initiate the play, have the attacker physically point to her feet to indicate that she is ready and wants the pass. And/or, she can point to her feet and yell, *"Feet!"* to her teammate as an extra measure of communication. Encourage the attacker to come out to meet/control the ball to begin her evasive dribbling and perform her turn. The attacker can control the ball with whatever surface she is most comfortable with, including the sole.

Because you are in a team training environment, the defender already knows what type of move the attacker is going to use, so caution her to be more passive in her defensive actions. Encourage the attacker to execute the Step-Over rigorously and take the ball away at an appropriate angle and speed to support her shot on goal. Think ahead! If the attacker wants to take her shot on goal with her dominant foot, she needs to initiate the Step-Over with her non-dominant foot.

This drill can produce a lot of standing around if you are not operating multiple stations, so try to setup a second group of players on the opposite goal if you have access to a full field for practice. Split players up with a 2-3 player queue beside the left post that will be the defenders. Position 2-3 players to serve as passers, and one in the middle as the receiving attacker. After each cycle has ended, the passer moves to attacker, attacker moves to defender, and defender to passer.

If you do have full-sized goals train on, use this opportunity to train your Goal Keepers. If you have a single goal, consider putting two of them in it at the same time. They can each guard a one-half of the goal and both get some action. If one or both have inclinations to be field players as well, make sure you rotate them into the rest of the drill.

COACHING POINT: Remember that the goal of this drill is to turn on the defender and take a shot as quickly as possible. This is one of those situations where players will want to stay on the ball 'just a little longer' to get a better shot. Reinforce to them every little extra moment that they take to get their shot off reduces the chance that it will happen. Coach them to not wait for the 'perfect moment' but rather take the shot when even the slightest window presents itself.

(20) 4v4+4N Possession – Reference basic drill from practice 7-1.

(20) 6v6 SSG - This is essentially the same game as in previous sessions with the added encouragement of getting them to try the most recent fakes that they have been learning. Use the glow ball if you have it.

Coaching Point: At the risk of sounding repetitive, remember to enforce the 40 second time-out for a kick-away. Make sure they know before the game begins that the 40 second rule applies. This is the most powerful tool in your box for training control and possession.

Practice 9-1 - Email and Pre-Work:

Hi Parents,

Tomorrow we will be working on a dribbling fake called 'La Croqueta' made famous by Dutch midfielder Michael Landrup and further popularized by Barcelona midfielder Andrés Iniesta.   This is a wickedly simple take-on move that we will work on in all of our remaining practices. Here is a short video, only 1:36 minutes long that I would like you to have your daughters watch so that they can see how the move is executed in a game:

Andres Iniesta's Signature Move – La Croqueta

https://www.youtube.com/watch?v=TbT3m4w4AL0

Additionally, here is a longer video of Iniesta's Barcelona teammate Lionel Messi using this move (and many more) to dribble through multiple defenders. This is one of the best H.D. productions of Messi dribbling that I have seen. The big take-away from this video is watching how Messi moves and keeps the ball right at the end of his feet. One moment he will be moving like lightening, the next he slows the game down and fakes defenders off their feet. It's a best-in-class style to be studied and adopted to the extent that any student of the game can. This video is a little longer, but very inspiring and well worth the watch:

Can Messi Actually Do Magic? Look At These 100 Ridiculous Skills By Him!

https://www.youtube.com/watch?v=aA7JaGZttuE

Practice 9-1: Dribbling circuit, La Croqueta (intro), change-of-direction, red light/green light

(15) Forward Fake Dribbling Circuit – Setup the 'Forward Fake Dribbling Circuit' as indicated in Practice 1-2. Your players will be performing step-overs through the circuit and taking the ball away using the outside of the foot. Keep the pace moderately slow to maintain control. Players should be using very small touches to move the ball from cone-to-cone.

The ball should be rolling when you do your fake; this will make it easier to perform your take-away as the ball will be rolling into a better position to take-away at the proper angle...which is about 40 degrees. If you stop the ball, the angle of take-away is going to be more of a sideways move where forward motion will be lost.

To give the players a better sense of timing the opposition, straddle the 2nd cone with a low defensive stance. Actively instruct your attacker to dribble straight at you so that she doesn't give away which way she intends to go. Offer no resistance at this point, but rather follow the direction of their fake so that they can experience what a successful take-away feels like. If you have plenty of coaching help, or other capable volunteers, position them at other cones throughout the circuit to offer the same passive-defending. Give plenty of corrections and praise as is warranted. Emphasize the step-over should be executed vigorously to really sell the fake. As you straddle the cone, make sure that you don't back into dribblers approaching your cone from the opposite direction.

This is first session that I used high-visibility (yellow), high-profile cones for the circuit. I could be imagining it, but it seemed that players did a little better job in executing their move before the larger cones than they did with the smaller ones. If you don't have large profile cones, it's not a big deal; just use the normal profile cones.

(20) Intro to La Croqueta – Introduction of the La Croqueta fake this late in the season represents more of a commitment to player development than it does training a near-term usable skill; You are *not* likely to see it in any of your last games of the season. That doesn't mean you won't, though! It just depends upon how aggressively your most talented players practice at home.

This is a skill that you want to break-down into multiple progressions for your inexperienced players. From a stationary position, start by introducing the basic movement of dragging the ball across the body with one foot and touching it forward with the inside of a properly angled opposite foot. This angle is approximately 45 degrees and can be thought of as a bumper on a billiards table that deflects the ball into the forward direction. The trick to pulling off this fake is to execute it quickly and touch the ball forward as the swinging foot is coming back in contact with the ground. This is where the giant 'tick tocks' (a.k.a. 'foundations' or 'bell touches') practiced in earlier sessions will help with the required movement.

Following Figure 9-1, lay out enough stations of 3 cones (25" in width) to represent a defender. Station two players at each station. If you have an odd number of players, that's OK. The players will be starting with their right foot dragging the ball to their left foot to make a touch forward. The starting position of the ball needs to be about arms length out from the middle/right cone to represent pulling the ball across the defender's body. Make sure your players are not too close and not too far away from the cones (defender).

Intro to La Croqueta

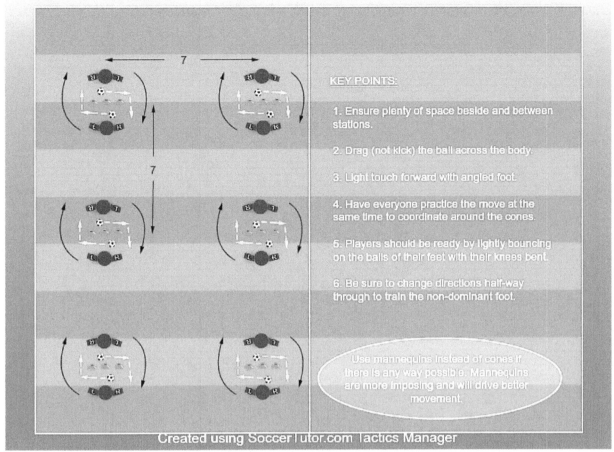

KEY POINTS:

1. Ensure plenty of space beside and between stations.

2. Drag (not kick) the ball across the body.

3. Light touch forward with angled foot.

4. Have everyone practice the move at the same time to coordinate around the cones.

5. Players should be ready by lightly bouncing on the balls of their feet with their knees bent.

6. Be sure to change directions half-way through to train the non-dominant foot.

Use mannequins instead of cones if there is any way possible. Mannequins are more imposing and will drive better movement.

Created using SoccerTutor.com Tactics Manager

Figure 9-1

How to execute the move: This instruction is for execution to the left. Be sure to practice the move in the opposite direction. Start by straddling the ball (shoulder width) with the players' toes even with the edge of the ball. The ball should be about 2-3 inches from the inside of the right foot. Begin by shifting weight to the left foot, simultaneously hop off the left foot while dragging the ball across the body with the right, and take a touch forward with the left foot *before* it hits the ground. The touch forward needs to be strong enough (4-5 feet) to sprint onto the ball to beat the defender. This fake is typically executed at a moderate pace, but the change-of-speed after the fake should be blistering in order to beat the defender.

As with the other moves you have instructed, encourage your players to practice these moves at home with any simple (unbreakable) object to serve as a defender.

You can do an Internet search on the following phrase and find many good examples for instructing the La Croqueta soccer move: SOCCER LA CROQUETA TUTORIAL VIDEO

(20) Escape – This drill encourages players to use the fakes they have been learning to change direction and escape from a circle with four exits guarded by 3 defenders. This drill forces your players to get their 'head up' to see where the open exit is and plan their escape. It also promotes agility on the part of the defenders as they must be continually paying attention and quickly adjust to the movements of the attacker.

Escape

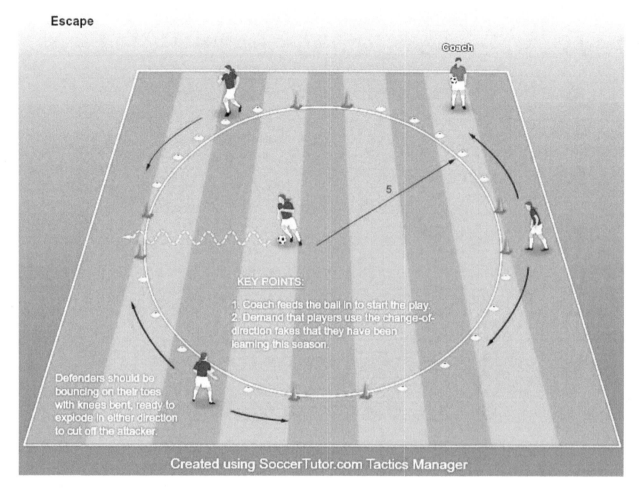

Figure 9-2

Following Figure 9-2, setup a 10-yard diameter circle with 4 exits about 1 yard wide. Setup as many stations as you have players to support. Get creative if you are short a player by making one of the circles with 3 exits guarded by 2 defenders. If you have one too many, consider a bigger circle with 5 exits. The more players you can keep engaged the more productive your training will be.

Quickly assign the defenders and an attacker to the circle. Begin with the coach playing the ball into the attacker to start her dribble/escape. Encourage the defenders to be lower to the ground and on the balls of their feet to adjust quickly to the attacker. The defenders will initially try to guard the exits directly, which is less effective than splitting the distance between two exits, so encourage them to *not* guard the exit.

As the coach, be vocal and demand that you want to see them using the lunge, pull-back, cut behind standing leg, and step-over fakes that they have been learning this season. Emphasize that they can only escape by dribbling out of an exit, and not passing/kicking the ball out of the exit.

Don't rotate players into the middle too quickly. Let each player have a few turns trying to escape before you rotate another player in.

(25) 6v6 SSG on Short field - Reference basic drill from Practice 3-1. Use the Glow Ball if you have one.

<u>Coaching Point:</u> Remember to enforce the 40 second time-out for a kick-away! Make sure they know before the game begins that the 40 second rule applies. This is the most powerful tool in your box for training control and possession.

(10) Red Light/Green Light – Reference basic drill from Practice 2-2.

Practice 9-2: Dribbling circuit, La Croqueta (passive), pattern passing, turning, 6v6 SSG

(10) Forward Fake Dribbling Circuit – Setup the 'Forward Fake Dribbling Circuit' as indicated in Week 1-2. Train step-overs taking away with the outside of the foot identical to last practice 9-1.

(20) La Croqueta Against Static Defender – La Croqueta Progression – Dribble on a mannequin or live (but static) player and perform the fake on-the-move.

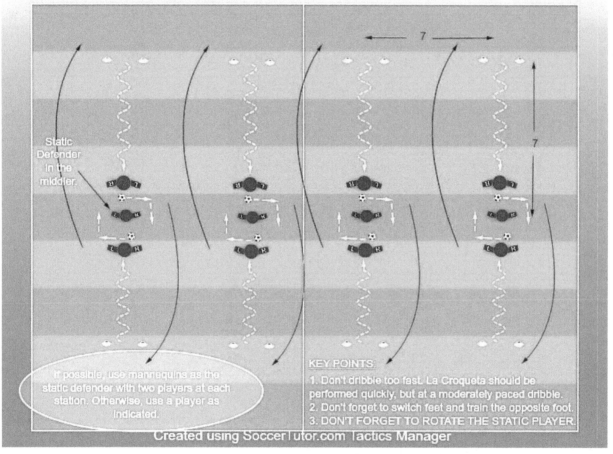

Figure 9-3

(15) Run-Through Triangles - One of the most challenging behaviors to train young players is movement 'off of the ball.' Early in the season we trained the '3 step rule' where a player that passes the ball to a teammate must move at least three steps in a direction that allows support for the player receiving the ball. The term 'Support' means being in the right place at the right time to support the attack. In the context of the '3 step rule', this means being available for a pass back if the receiver gets into trouble. This drill is designed to further train 'moving into space' in a bigger way that helps develop ball handling skills while on-the-move.

Following the pattern in Figure 9-4, provide a demonstration with a group of your best passers for the rest of the players to watch. If you have a full field to train on, start a triangle of passers about 7-8 yards apart on the goal line like an arrow pointing up the field. If you don't have a full field, play across the half in the same manner. Player A will start with the ball and begin the sequence by passing to Player B. Immediately after passing to Player B, Player A *sprints* into space between players B and C to move the triangle up the field. As Player A arrives into position to reestablish the triangle shape, Player B then passes to Player C. Player B then makes her run in-between Players A and C. The passing sequence continues on a diagonal path toward the opposite corner of the field given the nature of the run-throughs.

Run-Through Triangles

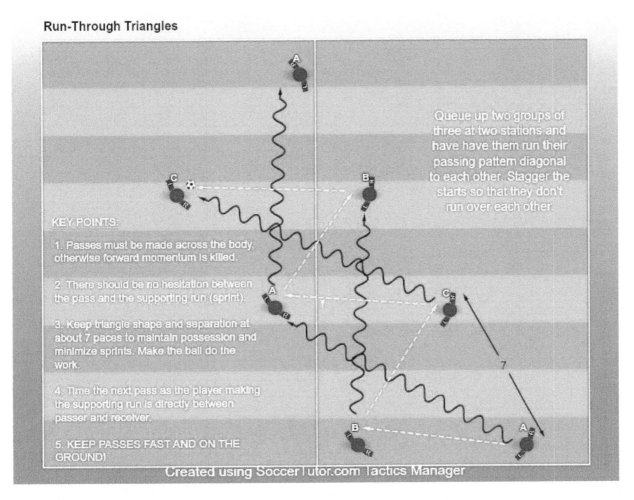

KEY POINTS:

1. Passes must be made across the body, otherwise forward momentum is killed.

2. There should be no hesitation between the pass and the supporting run (sprint).

3. Keep triangle shape and separation at about 7 paces to maintain possession and minimize sprints. Make the ball do the work.

4. Time the next pass as the player making the supporting run is directly between passer and receiver.

5. KEEP PASSES FAST AND ON THE GROUND!

Queue up two groups of three at two stations and have have them run their passing pattern diagonal to each other. Stagger the starts so that they don't run over each other.

Created using SoccerTutor.com Tactics Manager

Figure 9-4

Instruct your players that they will want to take at least two touches on the ball to allow their teammate running through the middle enough time to re-establish the triangle shape. As they learn to adjust to the movements of their teammates, you will see some players make a one-touch pass to the next receiver and take the legs out from under the runner. These are the times you will want to make these verbal corrections to help them improve their play.

Another critical aspect of this drill is making passes in the forward direction across the body of the receiver. Emphasize that the passer needs to take enough time on the ball to execute a good pass in front of her teammate and not behind her. Make it clear that a pass behind the next player receiving the ball KILLS the momentum of the attack because the receiver must turn around in the direction of her own goal in order to control the ball. Keep the play moving forward!

(25) 1v1 Defender on Back – Reference basic drill from Practice 8-2.

(20) 6v6 SSG Unstructured– Reference basic drill from Practice 3-1. Use the Glow Ball if you have one.

<u>Coaching Point:</u> Remember to enforce the 40 second time-out for a kick-away! This is the most powerful tool in your box for training control and possession.

Practice 10-1 - Email and Pre-Work:

Subject Line: Practice before practice and a reminder

Hi Folks,

We will be working on the La Croqueta move again tomorrow night. Last week we introduced/practiced this move from a static start position to keep it simple. Last night we graduated to dribbling slowly at a static defender and executing the move. Tomorrow night, in the spirit of Halloween, we are going to practice this move while Zombie Dodging. Using the La Croqueta move, the Dribblers will have to evade Zombies mindlessly marching toward them in a tight channel.

If your daughter wants to practice a little more tonight to avoid becoming a Zombie too quickly, here is another great tutorial for the La Croqueta move that they would benefit from watching:

La Croqueta ~ Iniesta's Signature Move - Online Soccer Academy

< Insert current link to this or another online tutorial of your choice >

For those of you that are pursuing Club soccer in the Spring, I would highly recommend that you enroll your daughter in one of the Winter Coerver® programs that I referenced in an earlier email.

Time just zooms by; It's hard to believe that our last game is on Saturday.

Thanks,
Coach Scott

Practice 10-1: Sharks/minnows, zombie dodging, pattern passing, 4v4+GK transition, and 6v6 SSG

(10) Sharks & Minnows – This is a fun and chaotic variant on the game commonly known as 'sharks and minnows.' Put all players (except one), with their own ball, into an area of 15x20 yards (or adult paces). These players will be the minnows. Start one player inside the area without a ball. This will be the first 'shark'. On your command of "Go!", the shark will try to kick as many balls out of the area as possible. If a player has her ball knocked out of the area, she then becomes a shark. Play is continuous down to the last player in possession of a ball. This area gives players plenty of area to move the ball and work their moves.

(20) Zombie Dodging – Just in time for Halloween! This is a progression of the La Croqueta fake that we have been training for the last 2 practices. After having performed the fake against a static defender, this fun exercise introduces (very) passive resistance with slow moving Zombie Defenders lurching toward the attackers in a narrow channel.

Zombie Dodging

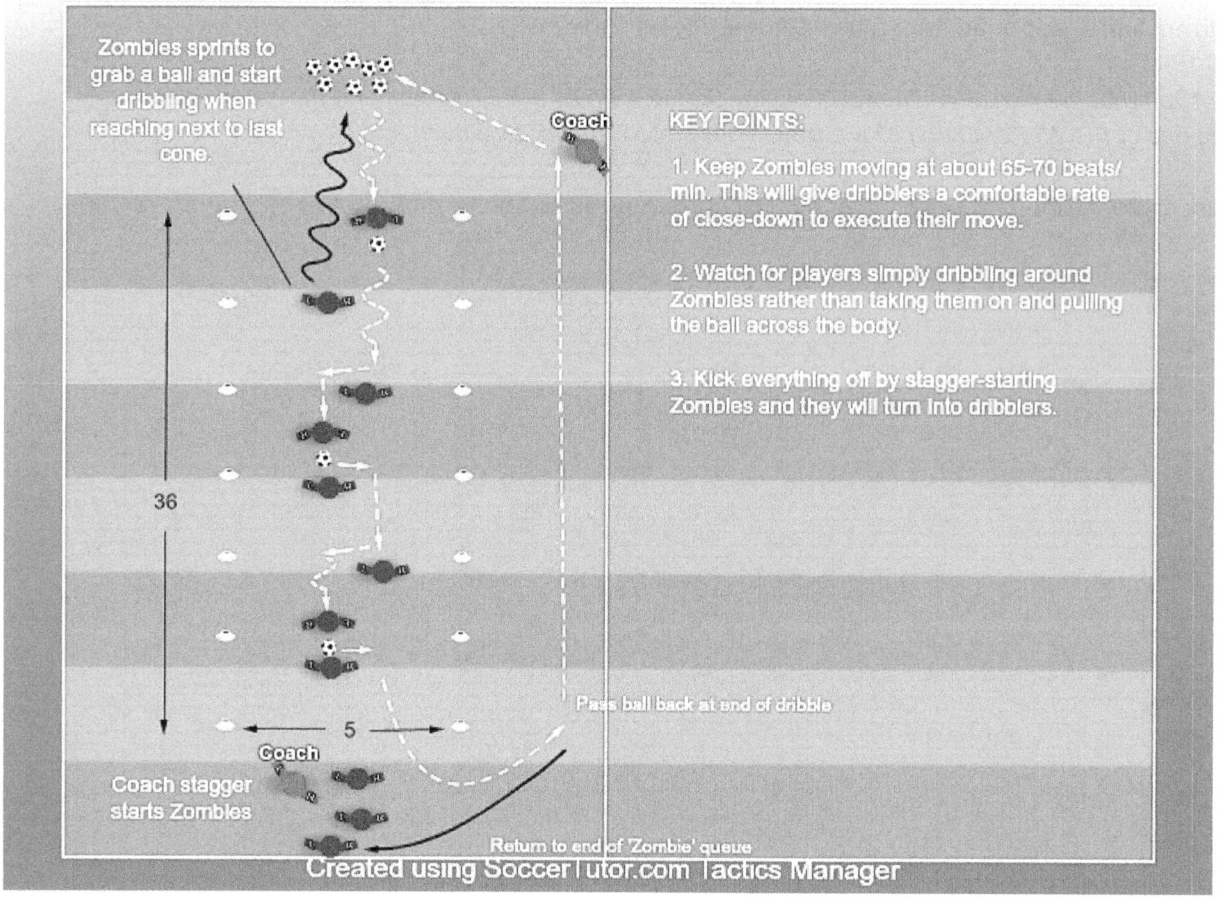

Zombies sprints to grab a ball and start dribbling when reaching next to last cone.

Coach

KEY POINTS:

1. Keep Zombies moving at about 65-70 beats/min. This will give dribblers a comfortable rate of close-down to execute their move.

2. Watch for players simply dribbling around Zombies rather than taking them on and pulling the ball across the body.

3. Kick everything off by stagger-starting Zombies and they will turn into dribblers.

36

5

Pass ball back at end of dribble

Coach

Coach stagger starts Zombies

Return to end of 'Zombie' queue

Created using SoccerTutor.com Tactics Manager

Figure 10-1

Following Figure 10-1, lay out a channel 5 paces wide by approximately 36 paces long with a cone drop every 6 paces. Position all players in a queue on one end of the channel and all of the balls near the opening of the opposite end. If you are 'over the top' like I am, download a metronome app on your phone and play 65-70 beats/minute over your portable 100w speaker! If you don't have these tools, you can thump the back of a pot or crack a couple of sticks together to control cadence. Or, do nothing at all.

Have your assistant coach manage introduction of the players into the channel and do their best 'walking dead' impression with their arms held out and making zombie noises while they walk. It sounds silly, but a bunch 10-11 year old players will love it. Have the coach introduce the next Zombie when the one in front reaches the first 6-yard cone. As each Zombie clears the next to the last cone, she races to the end, grabs a ball, and becomes a star La Croqueta dribbler (like Landrup and Iniesta) in the opposite direction. When the dribbling player clears the last Zombie, she passes her ball back to the opposite end goes to the back of the Zombie queue.

As the coach, help keep the balls available and continually provide corrections to the dribblers. Watch for dribblers not taking the ball across the body of the defender. Many will simply dribble to the side and not perform the fake at all. Require that they pull the ball across the body and perform the fake. Some will not strike the ball in the continuous 'tick tock' fashion before the receiving foot touches the ground. Keep pointing out and correcting these behaviors in a positive manner. It might sometimes seem like you are wasting your breath, but they need to keep hearing it until they get it right.

Very importantly, remind them that they are learning and that this is not a race. Have them slow down the dribble to a speed that they can comfortably execute the fake and be successful. These are the early stages of learning this move and it requires a lot of patience from coaches and players alike.

(20) Run-Through Triangles – Reference basic drill from Practice 9-2.

(20) 4v1+GK Transition - This is transition drill, meaning that the focus is on what happens when a team loses or gains control of the ball. The layout of the drill forces positional play and anticipation of the transition.

As indicated in Figure 10-2, lay out a short field of approximately 20x40 yards with a line of cones marking the midpoint line. Play with full-size goals if you have access to them. If not, position two Pugg-style mini-goals 8 yards apart on the touchlines and play across the field. Approximately 10 yards out from each post, position a cone-gate about 2 yards wide that attackers must play through *before* they can take a shot on goal. This little aspect of the game forces major amounts of control, passing, and movement off-the-ball. Otherwise, you will have a lot of errant shots on goal that constantly take the ball out of play. Shots on goal are a good thing, but this is a possession exercise and getting your players to cooperate in the attack is the training objective. If you disagree about taking the shot from distance, simply pull the cone-gates up and let them shoot at their first opportunity.

Four Blue attackers will be restricted to Red's side of the field and Blue will have one lone defender in its defensive half. Red has the opposite configuration. Put players who normally play Keeper in the goals so that they can field some shots. If you have the odd player, just add them to the weaker attacking side.

Start the play by simply feeding the ball out to one set of attackers. Play becomes ongoing after a goal or a miss; just have the Keeper play the ball to her teammates on the other side of the field. No punts allowed...only kicks off the ground or throwing.

4v1+GK w Transition

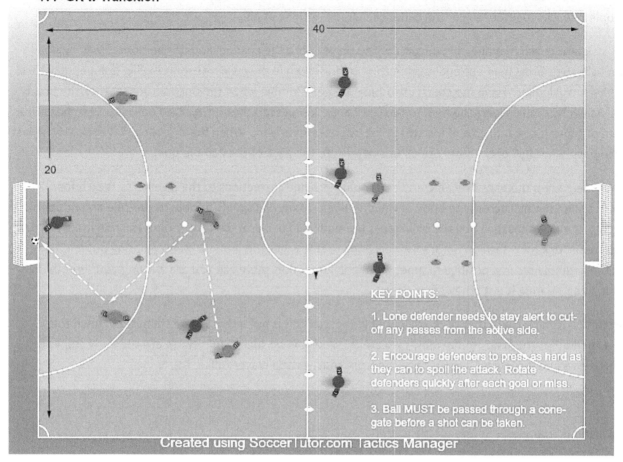

KEY POINTS:

1. Lone defender needs to stay alert to cut-off any passes from the active side.

2. Encourage defenders to press as hard as they can to spoil the attack. Rotate defenders quickly after each goal or miss.

3. Ball MUST be passed through a cone-gate before a shot can be taken.

Created using SoccerTutor.com Tactics Manager

Figure 10-2

This drill is purposely designed for the attackers to be successful. This means that the lone defender is going to be working her tail off to pressure the ball in her defensive half. With this in mind, make sure you rotate defenders after each goal.

The lone defender's role is *not* to 'clear' the ball (i.e., kick it out of bounds), but rather win it from the attackers and play it to one of her teammates on the other side. This represents a transition. The lone defender on the inactive side of the field must be paying close attention to play and be ready to intercept any pass from the other teams Defender. This translates to anticipating and responding to when the ball is lost and which attacker is most likely to receive any attempted pass. If your players are not intuitively moving in this manner, give them guidance.

(20) 6v6 SSG - Reference basic drill from Practice 3-1. Use the Glow Ball if you have one.

Coaching Point: Remember to enforce the 40 second time-out for a kick-away! This is the most powerful tool in your box for training control and possession.

Epilogue

This teaching plan is presented as 'A' plan for your season and not 'THE' plan by any stretch of the imagination. When I first started coaching, I found most of the readily-available references for training methods and philosophies to be too Cookbook-ish and less like the navigational 'roadmap' that I was looking for. So, for nearly a year before my first U-10 season, I asked myself the fundamental questions of *"What should players really be learning and when?"* and *"How should they be taught?"* I also had to ask this within the context of what my daughter and her teammates were ready for. What you see in this plan is the distillation of this research, influenced by my own inexperience and personal biases. This is what makes it an imperfect plan and not the 'holy grail' of training that each of us would like to stumble upon. While imperfect, this plan has helped me produce a positive experience for those in my little soccer universe and I hope you can use it to do the same.

Please accept my apologies in advance for the numerous references to training that had been conducted in the previous season. I have found this first experience of writing a full-season plan to be similar to jumping into a river. Like the more attractive spot just a little farther up the river to jump in, there is always something more preliminary to be taught. So, I've decided to just take the plunge and present Volume 2 with the apology that there is no Volume 1 at the time of this writing. If this plan is found to be more useful than not, perhaps a Volume 1 will follow.

Appendix A – Coaches Equipment Bag

Coaches Field Equipment:

12 - Large Profile (6") Cones w/ wire carrier

16 - Standard Profile Blue Cones (various drills)

45 - Standard Profile Orange Cones w/ wire carrier (for various drills)

6 - Blue pinnies (for 6v6)

13 - Orange Pinnies (for full scrimmage and 6v6)

4 - Green Pinnies (for 4v4v4)

4 - Red Pinnies (for 4v4v4)

12- Coaching sticks (2 sets of 6)

3-6 - Heading Trainer Balls (or equivalent) TheTrainingTriangle.com

2 - American Football-style Strike Pads (or seat cushions from your couch)

1 - Glow-in-the-Dark Soccer Ball (Size #5 is OK)

1 - 40" Giant Soccer Ball (you may have to pool resources with another coach for this one)

1- Bullhorn (for red light/green light) Not required, but fun.

2 – Approx. 14' lengths of agility ladder

1 - 50' section of 5/8" UnManila rope for Tug-O-War and Jump Rope

4 - 9" Red or Orange Cones

4 - mini goals (Pugg-Style)

Make sure you use Youth-Large Pinnies. I have seen some coaches use adult Pinnies that are constantly falling off and become a terrible distraction. Players are constantly adjusting the Pinnie instead of focusing on their play.

Coaches Bag:

1 - Under Armour dual action ball pump and extra needles

3 - Extra #4 balls (1 for you and 2 for your players that forgot theirs)

2 - Stopwatches (for timing sprints and dribbling exercises)

2 - Pair of Keeper gloves (1 pair Size #7 and 1 pair Size #5) for players to try out.

2 - Instant Ice Compress packs

1 - Pair extra shoelaces (and a couple extra pair of old cleats of appropriate sizes if you are able)

1 - Pack various band-aids

1 - Extra pair of shin guards. Like the Nike™ Mercurial Lite that slip quickly under the sock

2 – Whistle

2 - Hand click-counters (for measuring ball-touches, keeping score, etc.)

1 - Pack of extra hair bands (no floppy hair allowed!)

3 – Different colored Pinnies for Goal Keeper color conflicts

Bonus Equipment: Portable speaker to play music during fun activities and toward end-of-season 6v6.

Bibliography

Introduction

Wooden, J. and Jamison, S., 2005. *Wooden On Leadership*. New York: McGraw-Hill, p.242.

Wooden, J. and Jamison, S., 2005. *Wooden On Leadership*. New York: McGraw-Hill, p.22.

Dashwood. (2012). Hours for Teaching and Preparation Rule of Thumb: 2-4 Hours of Prep for 1 Hour of Class. Retrieved 12 June 2020, from http://americanfacultyassociation.blogspot.com/2012/02/hours-for-teaching-and-preparation-rule.html#:~:text=%22Most%20teachers%20spend%20at%20least,Method%20Harvard%20Business%20School%20Press.

The 6 Commandments of Every Practice

Wooden, J. and Jamison, S., 2005. *Wooden On Leadership*. New York: McGraw-Hill, p.156.

Schwartz, D. (2012). *The magic of thinking big*. New York: Simon & Schuster.

Week 1

Tooby, D., 2015. *Soccer Skills - How To Communicate In Soccer - Soccer Tips*. [online] www.progressivesoccertraining.com. Available at: <https://www.youtube.com/watch?v=IZjE2OY_y6o> [Accessed 5 April 2020].

Blank, D. (2012). *Soccer IQ* (p. 19).

Week 2

Pranjic, J., 2020. *The Benefits Of Teaching And Rehearsing Throw-In Choreography. [Coaching 04] - 3Four3*. [online] 3four3. Available at: <https://343coaching.com/podcast/soccer-by-3four3/benefits-teaching-rehearsing-throw-choreography-coaching-04/> [Accessed 2 May 2020].

Lemov, D., Woolway, E. and Yezzi, K., 2012. *Practice Perfect*. San Francisco, Calif.: Jossey-Bass, p.53.

Week 3

Wojack, B. (2020). Soccer Formations and Systems as Lineup Sheet Templates - Brant Wojack. Retrieved 7 May 2020, from https://www.brantwojack.com/Home/Lineups

Sumpter, D. (2017). *Soccermatics*. London: Bloomsbury Publishing Plc.

Week 5

USYS. (2019). POLICY ON PLAYERS AND PLAYING RULES. Retrieved 3 June 2020, from http://www.usyouthsoccer.org/assets/56/6/us_youth_soccer_policy_on_players_and_playing_rules.pdf

Week 6

Toledo, P. (2020). The Secret Behind Lionel Messi's Devastating Dribbling Style. Retrieved 12 May 2020, from https://the18.com/soccer-learning/lionel-messi-dribbling-style-explained-drills

Made in the USA
Las Vegas, NV
26 August 2021